左手外贸 右手英语

TRADING EMAIL TEMPLATE ANAYLSIS

朱子斌 著

机械工业出版社
China Machine Press

图书在版编目（CIP）数据

左手外贸右手英语 / 朱子斌著 . —北京：机械工业出版社，2018.7（2025.5 重印）

ISBN 978-7-111-60448-8

I. 左… II. 朱… III. 对外贸易－英语 IV. F75

中国版本图书馆 CIP 数据核字（2018）第 147543 号

    这不是一本教你英语的书。本书教的，是怎样用英语去做国际贸易。作者自毕业起迄今 20 年的时间内，一直都在中国制造贸易行业做销售或采购工作，对贸易有十分深的见解。本书结合他在 500 强企业工作期间，以及他和朋友经历过的实际案例，讲述在外贸思维与英语思维碰撞下，如何成为一个出色的外贸高手。

    "价格、分销、品质、报价、交货期"，是每一个外贸人都要面对的重要事项，本书从正确的、错误的、常规的、高效的等不同维度，详细剖析怎么做才能顺利达成交易。作者还特别介绍了如何跟客户搞好关系，怎样写好文案。在最后，还有你一定会非常喜欢的模板和工具，略作修改就可立即在实务中应用（读者购书且在朋友圈晒书后，加微信号 lsmeihua 领取）。

左手外贸右手英语

出版发行：机械工业出版社（北京市西城区百万庄大街 22 号）   邮政编码：100037

责任编辑：刘新艳   责任校对：殷　虹

印　　刷：河北虎彩印刷有限公司

开　　本：170mm×230mm　1/16   版　　次：2025 年 5 月第 1 版第 20 次印刷

书　　号：ISBN 978-7-111-60448-8   印　　张：11

    定　　价：45.00 元

客服电话：（010）88361066　68326294

版权所有 · 侵权必究
封底无防伪标均为盗版

亲爱的读者！

感谢阅读本书，希望书中所讲内容，为你的工作和生活提供有益帮助。

你的好朋友正在寻找好书。赶快拿起你的手机，拍下本书的①封面、②封底、③你很喜欢的书中的内文、④其他希望得瑟的图片，拍出9张图，发到朋友圈。

1. 提供分享朋友圈截图，领取工具包，内含：

 - 20封邮件模板（word格式）
 - 36条外贸金句

2. 提供朋友圈截图，加入外贸英语微信群，一起交流和分享专业问题。

本书编辑的微信号：huh88huh；昵称：胡小乐；

加好友时备注：外贸英语。

出版图书或购书，欢迎联系我！

祝大家工作顺利！

扫一扫二维码，加胡小乐的微信

前言

这不是一本教你英语的书。我教的,是怎样用英语去做国际贸易。

事实上,要做好外贸,你要学的绝对不只是英语。试想想,要是英语是外贸中最重要的一环,那么那些在中国的老外为什么还在做英语外教,应该都跑去做外贸了吧。

从 1999 年毕业起至成书的 18 年间,我一直在中国制造外贸行业工作,而且绝大部分岗位都是采购。这些年来,我收到了大量"开发信",也经手了很多因沟通不畅而坏了事的订单。身为买方的我深深体会到问题的核心远远不只是没有用好英语,而是背后的商业思维问题。当出现一个重大的质量问题,你在 ×× 英语培训机构学的那些短句,那些你天天打卡背的单词,有多少真的能帮上你?

我国为出口大国、世界工厂,可惜却没有系统的外贸英语教育。学校教的是基础英语,市面上的培训机构教的是职场英语。零零散散的有个别人士提供了一些外贸专用英语的参考，然而也是杯水车薪，聊胜于无。20岁出头的外贸员面对经验老到的"中国通"老外买家，在买卖关系、人生经验强弱分明的情况下，如果连有效的英语沟通都做不到，那只能在国际贸易中扮演最底层的劳力或搬运工的角色，干最苦的活，赚最少的钱。

商务英语（business English），顾名思义，是先商务（business），后英语（English）。在本书中，你会看到一个跟你目前所学完全不同的贸易和英语的思维系统，你会看到一个世界制造业500强出身的人怎样运用语言达到商业目的。我特别希望本书能让读者看清楚学习英语的本质，不要盲目浪费时间和金钱学一些跟你的目标无关的知识。文法不好、单词不够，都不是你做不好外贸的原因。

《左手外贸右手英语》（原称《本叔的商业英语》）从2016年年初开始，在微博、阿里外贸圈等平台连载，好评如潮。承蒙机械工业出版社华章分社支持，30篇的内容终能成书。感谢一直以来"外贸G友团"几位好兄弟的支持，感谢毅冰老师的穿针引线，同时感谢几位热心的读者协助粗心大意的我完成校对工作。最后，必须感谢我太太的支持，照顾好我和女儿，让我能在很多个晚上专心写作。

P.S. 如果你需要书中部分邮件内容的电子文档，请购书且在微信朋友圈晒书后，加微信号lsmeihua领取。

目录

前言

第1章 价格 /1

如何应对客户索要的促销价格 /3
You are too expensive 怎么破解 /8
我已经尽了最大努力 /12
Price, or pricing /18
除了钱你们就不能聊些别的吗 /22
因为原材料涨价我也要涨了,该怎么写 /29
有没有遇到过客户拿着几年前的报价单来跟你下单 /34

第2章 分销 /40

如何应对包销 /41
总有老外想与我合作 /47

第 3 章　品质 / 57

客户由于质量问题不付款怎么办（1）/ 58
客户由于质量问题不付款怎么办（2）/ 62
质量投诉该如何处理 / 66
八级英语为什么写不出好 BE / 71

第 4 章　报价 / 76

这是真客户吗 / 77
如何解释报价 / 83
DDU 怎么谈才好 / 90

第 5 章　交货期 / 98

厦门刮台风，不可抵抗与只懂说不的客户 / 99
如何对待指鹿为马的客户 / 105

第 6 章　关系 / 113

客户想把你的产品美照借为己用怎么办 / 115
客户终于发现我一直在坑他，怎么破解 / 121
侵权？我打劫你家其实也挺辛苦的 / 128
本叔不会写开发信，但"再开发信"
　还是可以说一说的 / 133
关于飞单这件事，我是如何
　脸也不红地跟老外解释的 / 137

新年第一单，不拿白不拿 / 142

第 7 章 文案 / 146

网站上的"关于我们"怎么写 / 147

如何给国营老企业写出爆款英文文案 / 152

网站文案如何写 / 155

第 8 章 工具 / 159

看厂报告之总结 / 160

邮件之外的 BE：简报的思路 / 165

REALLY GOOD NEWS
YOU WANT TO EXPAND YOUR MARKET

第1章 价 格

礼貌、四平八稳、没感情、没套近乎,这是典型的中式英文!
人家都把整盘大计告诉你了,你怎么还不夸夸客户想法多、真聪明?

商务英语（business English，BE）中探讨频率最高的话题，到目前为止，恐怕还是买卖双方在价格上的拉锯。有时，我会被大家的认真和天真所触动。想象一下：一个老外只要群发10个询盘，然后对每一个供应商都回复一句"you are too expensive"，你就随即感谢他的"kind reply"，并且立马傻傻地给他减价10%。结果过了一个星期老外还没有回复，你便又开始怀疑是不是价格还是太高，于是又去问对方有没有什么能为他效劳的？

这个问题怎么破解？我的唯一答案是：差异化，让价格帮你找到你真正的客户。要是你只想做一个国际搬运工，别人怎么卖你就怎么卖的话，说实话，本书帮不了你太多。

应对新客户和那些因为觉得你的报价太高就连样板都不想看的客户，我认为还是有些套路可言的。套一套目标价（直接问！没什么不好意思的，最多就是对方不回复你而已），打开天窗说亮话。"不是不能减价，看你的量啊"，这个基本套路，第1章第一部分是个很好的例子。我也看到不少网友直接拿它当作模版套用。值得注意的是，问目标价是可以的，但不要去问对方的目标利润。虽说你大概也能推算出来，但这是不礼貌的。这一点可参考第1章第四部分。

文化差异带来的影响比你想象中来得深远。很多在我们的社会中看似善意的事，有可能在老外眼中是不可思议甚至难以理解的。举个例子，有些人爱说"我提成也不要了就想跟你合作"。西方资本主义价值观中的一个思想就是"利己心"，没利的事谁做呀。另一个常见的例子，"我跟老板聊了一下，我们给你打个八折吧"……请问你是在市场卖菜吗？

在20世纪90年代的深圳罗湖商业城吗？B2B（business to business）、OEM（original equipment manufacture）的报价都应该是有根有据、有公式的，而不是可以随意一减再减的。减价，也最好附上一个合理的理由。

第1章第三部分是我在2016年奥运会时写的，在用词的解释上，这部分也相当多，参考性也很强。

要是杀价杀得眼红，双方在价格上僵持不下，另一个上好的策略是不要只谈价格，尽量找出你和对手的区别，善加利用，扬长避短就对了。除了价格之外，难道你们之间就没什么别的可谈了吗？第1章第五部分提供了一个好例子。

其实围绕价格的话题还有很多，比如价格谈判中有哪些值得注意的细节。价格谈判也是大家非常关注的点，接下来会给大家提供更多这方面的案例做参考。

如何应对客户索要的促销价格

这是一个关于卖家跟客户合作做促销的例子。记得当年我的恩师曾说过一句话：在企业内，采购的力量来自供应商。除了日常的常规供货角色，供应商还是一个很好的资源，只是看你会不会利用。

这篇BE中的老外就很聪明，因为他懂得与供应商合作，一起去做促销。按照一般老板的OEM思维，你跟我买货了，你在你的市场里爱怎么玩就怎么玩，与我没有关系。可是在这些时刻，客户都会突然变身为你的长期伙伴，然后展露他纯真的笑容跟你要减价要钱："你好我好大家好啊！"

的确，促销是一件双赢的事，它很有可能为你带来更多的订单。拉拢供应商一块去承担风险确实是个好想法。下文是一封老外的邮件，大家可以学习一下对方是怎样说服供应商一起承担风险的。

I need a rock bottom price[1] for 500 pairs of ×× samples so I can use them for a direct mail advertisement. I will mail only the R or the L with a coupon to order the other one and more.[2] If it works, I will continue the campaign across the US and order more of these samples.

They do not need any package - lose in one box is fine. They will need the new glue strips and the logo. I don't care about the color of ×× you use, as long as the only change in ×× used is the color.

Can you partner with us on this promotion and give us a sample price of $ ×× per pair and we will pay the shipping for the single box.[3]

So in the future if we order samples, we can order a case of 500 each time at ××

1. "rock"的表面意思是很硬的，修饰"bottom price"，用来表示最低价。
2. 这招挺不错，一双鞋只寄一只，顾客试用了感觉良好再买另一只。
3. "partner with us"，你们都要成为我们的伙伴了。要人家减价的时候总是表现得那么的亲切。

each and you can pick the ×× color. This promotion will ask the lady to take the ×× challenge. Try it in one shoe...then we will give them a coupon to buy one at regular price and get the other sample L or R one free.

If it works we can pick up many clients and reorder more regular packages with you, but I need a partner[1] to help me lower the price for promotion. In US a mail promotion is usually 2% return, so we would take a chance to lose money on the first one.

If this is agreeable, I'm ready to pay the invoice.

然后是网友的回应。

Hello, ××:

It is a really good news you want to expand your market. As you know we always support with your team.[2]

But for this time base on two points we cannot do this way:

Ⅰ. MOQ issue, even no color limited, but every color we have MOQ when we purchase raw materials.[3] We have no raw materials in

1. 客户其实挺有诚意，开口闭口"partner"，他敢让你免费送他一批样板一起把市场做大。

2. 礼貌、四平八稳、没感情、没套近乎，这是典型的中式英文！人家都把全盘大计告诉你了，你怎么还不夸夸客户想法多、真聪明？

3. 这一句可改为：MOQ issue: When we purchased raw material we have MOQ limitation by color.

stock.

Ⅱ. Price issue, upon 500 pairs USD×× it is hard for us keep profit balance.[1]

But we have solution, we still have your color materials in our factory, we can produce 500 pairs use your materials.

Price we can make an discount for ××% without package.

If you have any comment pls let me know.

参考范文如下。

Hi ××,

Look like you have an innovative marketing campaign, I am interested in knowing how you came up with this idea?[2] As your supplier we certainly would work out a solid plan.[3]

Looking into the details I am afraid[4] there are 2 points that we might need to come over.

Ⅰ. MOQ: When we purchase from the factory they request an order with MOQ by color. Put it simple, one color, one MOQ.

Ⅱ. Target price: That is gonna be a very

1. 这样写也可以，不过直言是因为自己赚不够真的好吗？看你跟客户的关系了，这不一定是坏事。

2. 夸！人都喜欢被夸奖，这是个心理科学。再者，要是他真的跟你透露他的计划详情，这对你了解当地市场会有很大帮助。

3. "solid plan"可译为一个实际的计划。

4. 此处"afraid"不是真的怕，这是英文一个普通的用法，译作"恐怕"最适合。

challenging[1] target price to hit. Are you open for ideas about cutting the cost? For example, changing certain parts of the products…[2]

Good news is that we have some of your existing colors in stock and we could be flexible with those.

If you would like to go without packaging I am able to offer you an additional ××% discount.[3]

YES we are ready to receive your order. Let's keep the ball rolling.

Regards,

Ben

1. "challenging" 在这里表示很有挑战性的，暗示事情很难，你不要抱太大期望。
2. 这里在暗示另一件事，单纯的减价是不可行的，你一定要改一些东西让我的成本降下来，大家聊聊。
3. 注意减价百分比的设定，不要过高也不要过低。

本部分建议掌握的 BE 金句

1. work out a solid plan 制订一个翔实的计划

2. (Price) is very challenging /difficult. 表示价格难以达到对方期许。

3. Are you open for ideas about … 你是否愿意考虑（做某事）……

 （用于引导对方选择）

4. Let's keep the ball rolling. = Let's move on further.

You are too expensive 怎么破解

下面这个例子是阿里外贸圈的一个网友提供的。他的情况比较典型，他通过开发信找到客户，但客户说价格高，连样板都不想看就先来杀价。下文是来信的内容，删去商业机密信息，其他的原汁原味附上。

本叔，您好：

看了您发表在外贸圈的文章，我很受益，我是一个外贸新人，有一个关于样品和大货的价格谈不拢的客户，希望您帮我分析一下。

那位客户是我在阿里上认识的新客户，我们联系了一周，确定是买家。

我给客户发了CIF价格之后他没有回复，然后我说寄样品给他，他直接给了我地址，但是我说样品收费，结果他说我的大货价格贵，没必要买样品测试，就发过来下面这封邮件。

Hi J,

Your single price is out the budget, it is not worth purchasing the price. I am looking for ABS at $6.00 per kg landed in AAA (maybe $7.00). Your price is too high. It will be a waste to purchase your sample at $13.00.

你们为什么不觉得奇怪，这个$6是怎么来的呢？是客户编的，还是他用什么公式计算出来的？又或者是他从你的同行的报价得来的？本叔以15年的采购经验大声告诉你，这个所谓目标价有八成可能只是他随口说的！

Thank you.
Regards

夜里收到邮件我想了想还是回复吧,不然因为时差就会隔一天,隔夜联系感觉就不那么热乎了,可是我又觉得我的回复会让客户离我更远。

请本叔帮忙优化一下措辞。其实,我想表达的是市场上有价格便宜的,但肯定不是好货,只要有量,价格是可以谈的。以下是我的回复。

Hi ××,

Thanks for your kind reply.

其实我一直想说,人家就是来问个价,这有什么好"kind"的?就像打招呼,开篇就"dear",有什么好"dear"的呀?

We do not doubt that you can got offer price at \$7 or less CIF AAA from Chinese market.

We can also manufacture cheap cost product, however, it is unavoidably that printout success chance will go down and more after sales service request will come out. Which cost more time and not good for long-time cooperation.

这里我猜你是想说品质。

For final price, if you are satisfied with testing result and for following quantity price of 100, 500, 2000, 5000, I can ask a bottom price from my boss for you.

原来你报的不是底价,你还有很多空间,你在等我压价。我衷心地告诉你，一个专业的采购员看到你这个"bottom price"就会有我以上的反应了。

By the way, does your target price $6 (or $7) for every shipment no matter if the quantity 100, 500, 2000, or 5000 kg?

商业世界里，99%的价格都是跟数量挂钩的。

One of our regular customers from Australia choose us to be their filament supplier after one week China factory visiting. Welcome to visit us if you have time.

我想赞一下这段。客户参考（customer reference）用得不错，不过火候稍过，说得有点太神了。要知道看厂只是整个购买决策过程的一部分而已。

Thank you and best regards.

J

参考范文如下。

Hi,

Thanks for having a chance to review our quotation. The target price $6 seems challenging for us. May I know how do you come up with this target? I am very interested in knowing the magic behind and I would like to reasonably adjust it and try to match it.

We've seen products with unbelievably low price in local Chinese market, but I am not

一定要问！他可能真的有公式，这也是一个学习人家怎样做成本核算的好机会。反过来，如果这个目标价他是瞎掰的，有可能他就不再坚持。将心比心地想一想，"reasonably adjust"也表示我们的报价是有合理弹性空间的，而且我们是有诚意的。

sure we are talking in the same line. I believe you would agree that functionality, quality and after-sale services are key to success in our industry. We all know that a low price on the quotation could turn out to be never-ending trouble (and carrying cost, of course) in the future.[1]

Having said that, it is always our aim[2] to provide our customer with unparalleled quality product at affordable cost. What I would suggest is that let us review your annual product demands and come up with a price-volume mix for your reference. Communication is always the key to better support our customer.[3]

For your reference, YYY in your regional market has been our customer since long and it seems that Aussie[4] is quite satisfied with our product. Selling our product is proved to be profitable and reliable. I would be happy to tell you more about our activity in your market if you are interested.[5]

Let's keep the ball rolling.

Regards,

Ben

1. "I believe you would agree that..." "We all know that..." 这两个固定句式有"共情"的作用，目的是套近乎，用来表达我们的看法一致，同时也客气地暗示了"老外你难道不懂这个道理吗"。

2. 也可以用 we intended。

3. 看看我们如何高雅地表达"多买多优惠"，并且这里要懂得不忘自我宣传一下。

4. 假设是澳大利亚市场。

5. 这段话是全篇的画龙点睛之处，目的是激发老外和你进一步对话的欲望。老外一定有兴趣知道在他的市场上竞争对手的产品原来也是跟你买的，这表明你一定很懂对手的市场，也了解一些当地的法规。如此一来，谈下订单的机会又大了不少。

不过，话虽如此，还是不要太过迷信一封电邮就能改变世界。最后能不能成功斩获订单，靠的绝不只是几个英文字。

> **本部分建议掌握的 BE 金句**
>
> 1. May I know how do you come up with... I am interested in knowing the magic behind. 巧妙设问，探寻真相。
> 2. I believe you would agree that.../ We all know that... 表达共情，引导客户赞同我方看法。
> 3. A low price on the quotation could turn out to be never-ending trouble in the future. 报价单上显示的低价反而可能在将来意味着不少麻烦。

我已经尽了最大努力

这一部分我挑了一篇典型的中式英文。所谓的中式英文，是大家将花了无数时间死记硬背的英语单词，从小被英语老师纠正出来的语法，以及考试前夜挑灯夜战的各种应试笔记，综合起来机械地转换成一种带有明显汉语痕迹的英语。用中文思维写英文邮件，才是真真正正的硬伤。但好消息是，我们离开学校后要学的不是英国文学，不是莎士比亚。我们学英文是为了"用"，不是为了"炫"，你要懂的不是英式红茶的种类,不是美国共和党和民主党的差别。要写出好的 BE,你要懂的是西方的商业习惯和商业思维。这样一来学习的范围就缩小了,是不是对学好 BE 的信心大了很多?

下面是一个例子。

有一个英国的客户,他的购买意向很高,当时他有 25 000 英镑预算,但是我们的报价需要用好的材料,降价后也还差 3500 多美元,所以僵持住了。接着英镑贬值,差得就更多了,所以我们想出另一个方案,并报价给他,但按当时的汇率,还是超出客户的预算 2000 多美元。

客户一直没有反应,经询问,客户表示很快会下单,但是仍然希望我们降价。我跟老板沟通,决定满足客户的预算(是按汇率换过来的美元价),如下邮件不知道说的是否合理,但是客户到目前为止还没有回复,我们虽然有互动,但是没有谈及此事……

想问问本叔的意见!

1.
Dear,

　　I know you were busy these days.

　　Are you watching Olympics games?

　　With one of very popular Internet slang, " I have used my core power to obtain the new discount".

　　So I hope it could give you some help.

　　Thanks a lot! May I ask what's your opinion with the new prices?

看得出来你很努力地想要表现出不经意地问老外:"你看价格

可以吗？"既然老外问价时那么认真，你又花了那么多时间报价，其实客观来讲老外回一封邮件绝对是应该的。这时我们只要一句"how is the quotation"，提醒一下就足够了。

Best regards

2.
Dear ××,

Hope you all had a good weekend!

My Boss and sales manager had a meeting to discuss the YYY cases, also we talked about the aluminum material supplier to reduce the cost.

They agreed to give us 5% off on material within the next 10 days! It will be 3% off in total price. So we would like to give you this offer。

此处注意：这样你的原料成本比例就暴露了。这不一定有关系，但这和你公开给客户看的那个比例要对得上，不然就会被盘问。

In order to establish long term business relationship with you, my boss would like to show his greatest sincerity, he is willing to give up the only 5% profit.

我指的中文思维来了，这里真的是在挑战国际惯例！我很理解网友在国内可以在跟客户推杯换盏时说："我那5个点不赚了，都算你的好了，谁让咱们是好哥们。你信我吧！"然而，文化不同，老外听到的第一反应肯定是："你骗谁啊？没利润谁做啊？"另外，"long term business relationship, greatest sincerely"必须加上"as your best friend in China"，才能组成让老外调笑的三合一中式英语大招！

So there is new next 8% off for you totally.（This must be the lowest price this year we would offer.）

降低8%的成本是太高还是太低我不知道，行业各异，但有一点可以肯定的是，此文没有针对"客户是因汇率问题而来的成本痛点"做出反馈。你只是"跟老板开了个会""跟供应商聊了聊物料价"，然后，奇迹就出现了，8个点马上就能下来。记住：所有降价都必须有合理的理由，否则后面就有你受的了。相关主题的延伸读物是本叔写的"VE价值工程"一文。

We regard you as value as much, and please find the revised formal quotation as attached.

P.S. Because the supplier give us a time limited, so if you agree with new price, we are going to sign the material purchasing right now, and I will sent the PI for you soon.

这种"今天做特价，不买明天就没有了"真的不是B2B该有的思维，千万不要再这样写了！

Thanks and have good day!

Best regards,

J

以下是客户之前发来的邮件。单看内文，我认为连讲价都算不上，只是简单问问你还有什么可以做的吗，然后你轻轻松松就给出8个点的折扣，这会让客户产生"你还有多少骗了我"的想法。

3.

Hi J,

I'm sure we can do something. N, I'm sure will be in touch with you soon, like you we are all finding it hard this year, so anything you can discount would be great.

Kind regards

下面是最精彩的环节。单看老外这封邮件，这位网友实在不必急于降价。我在讲谈判时提过，沉默是高招。你看，这不就是最好的例子吗？对方若是再不说话，你是不是要再减10%？以下是参考范文。

Hi,

I am glad we are back to track eventually. We've been awaiting your feedback for long. As a matter of fact, we put quite some efforts to keep our offer valid up to the challenge of the recent currency fluctuation. I will explain.[1]

I am not sure we could offer you any further discount as you've got already our best offer.[2]

1. "我很高兴你终于回来了"，这句话带有轻微责怪的意味。我们还是该责怪他一下，不对吗？我们为他准备了这么多，他不在时我们仍然想尽办法帮他保持原价，他却走远了。记住，像一个人一样去聊天，像一个君子一样去问责，无可厚非。如果他有其他更好的选择，你说什么他都会走，懂吗？

2. "I am not sure"是非常好用的负面表达。这是所有美国人一听就懂的"no"这个词的客气版。

Be assured that the offer you've got is not something we will issue normally.[1] Yet, we understand the impact of the currency exchange rate could be a short term risk to you.[2] What we would like to suggest is that we adopt a price change mechanism.[3] Put it simple, the rule is that when the exchange rate is not in your favor, you'll get compensated; when the rate comes back to normal level, we will revert to our original offer. The attached document further explains it in details.

I wish that idea could strengthen your fate in our business.[4] Unfortunately, we have to attach a validity to this offer（as this is obviously our way to trigger the business launch）.[5]

I am available to talk with you online any time. Just give me a ring.

Regards,

Ben

1. "Be assured"的意思是：信我吧，没有骗你！
2. 强调"short term"的意思是：你不能用一个短期的风险来谈价格，大家都不傻，但我知道兄弟你也有难处，我们来想想办法。
3. 这是我常用的谈判手段。这里不详细说了，有机会在"假装在500强"系列里写一下。
4. 加强你对这个生意的信念。你不是在求他，而是在帮他成事，毕竟给你下单对他也是件好事。
5. 学问在这里！虽然我在上面提到，"今天做特价，不买明天就没有了"这个思维不好，可是我这里就用了。其实这个思路并非不可取，我在括号里特别补充的这句话想表达的意思是，要是你真的想用这个方法逼他早点下单，那么请你直接说。我们就是为了让你早点下单，怎么样？有时，光明正大做个小人也是一种手段。

> **本部分建议掌握的 BE 金句**
>
> 1. back to track 重回正轨 / 重回谈判桌
> 2. I am not sure that... 我不确定……
> 3. a price change mechanism 价格调整机制

Price, or pricing

这一部分比较轻松，也是属于"you are too expensive"系列，是大家最感兴趣的话题。我们就当作再一次复习吧。不过，这一篇有个值得注意的点。很多来稿网友反映出来的问题都是英文过关，但商业思维不行，但这位网友刚好相反，来稿逻辑不错，但英文表达不到位。网友原文如下。

我在和一个美国客户谈一款产品，我报了价格给他，他回复说产品贵暂时不考虑，邮件来回过程如下。

我：发了产品推广邮件给客户。

客户：询价……

我：询问客户的包装需求、数量。

客户：回复数量以及包装。

我：根据客户的数量做了详细报价给客户，并给了10%的折扣。

客户：说价格高。

我打算这样回复他：

1. 首先不否认客户觉得贵的意见，并且帮助他找出他觉得贵的原因。
2. 我想列出一般客户的产品价格构成，然后分析有哪些成本可以降低。
3. 我找了客户当地市场类似产品的价格进行对比，帮助客户分析怎样做才能在类似的产品中占据优势。

我在给客户分析他的产品价格构成时遇到了困难，我想表现得专业一些。

看到这里，我又忍不住想问一句，为什么动不动就打折？是因为数量，还是因为目标产品的规格？如果是这两个原因的话可以打折，但提醒大家千万不要在没有理由的情况下突然打折。

以下是网友的原文。

Dear A（又"dear"），

Thank you for your honest and valued comment.[1]

Well noted you think the pricing[2] is too high for you. You cannot get reasonable profit in your market with our quotations.

1. 人家就说你贵，没有什么 honest 不 honest 吧。也说不上这句错，但是不太适合。
2. 看下去，整篇都是用 pricing。大家知道 price 跟 pricing 的分别吗？

Never mind, let's find the reasons why the pricing we offered cannot have you make good profit.[1]

As a good and reliable supplier, we not only sell the products to customers, but more important is to help customers to sell their products in their market and make profit. OK, let's see if there are something we also can do and help.[2] Andrew, do you know the rough pricing for such kind of product in your market and do you have a general idea about what pricing can help you to sell the product well in your market?[3]

As I think, Your Final Pricing = Supplier Pricing + Shipping Cost + Duties and Taxes + Labor Cost + Reasonable Profit.[4]

1. 我仿佛看到一个任性少女被抛弃后拨弄一下头发说"never mind"，用在这里也不太恰当。不仅是表达太口语化的原因，而且感觉好像是对方做错了什么似的。
2. 好，你说得对，但太露骨了，也很难卖。
3. 估计你是想问：你那边这东西大概卖多少钱？你觉得什么价位能让你赚得够？英文的"price"当然是价格，但"pricing"是指定价。在这个例子里两个词都对，但你们用的时候必须知道区别！
4. 查完人家底细后你打算怎样做？由于原文没写完，后文也就不得而知了。

我必须同意，网友这个回复的逻辑是对的。大部分客户，特别是第一次接触时都会说你的价格贵。不管你是不是贵，总之你就是"too expensive"。你是什么反应？一上来就减个 10%？认真你就输了！网友这个做法是对的，不否认贵，解释贵的原因，成本都是什么，可是英文太差了。我只能说，看是看得明白，但写得不专业。是不是可以过关？嗯，我想是的。能不能更好？大有改进空间！

参考范文如下。

Hi,

Thanks for your reply and your concern regarding our price is well understood. As an OEM service provider, our success strongly relies on our customer's profitability and therefore we are willing to leave this open for further discussion. Yet, please understand that our offer is based on the actual cost of the material quality we have used and we are happy to explain to you further.

上面几句就把原文要说的内容说清楚了。下面就不写了，因为没有原文所以没法修改。不过，我不打算去问客户"要赚多少钱才够"这样一个太深入又可能让人感觉无礼（特别是在大家不熟的情况下）的问题。此等问题不是不能问客户，但前提必须是对方是你相当熟悉的合作伙伴。

本部分建议掌握的 BE 金句

1. Your concern regarding ×× is well understood.
2. We are willing to leave this open for discussion.

除了钱你们就不能聊些别的吗

这一部分中又是一篇"you are too expensive"类的文章。这种例子层出不穷,回应的手段却有一些套路可以应用。多看案例,越看你就会越精明。看完本书后好好总结,相信今后再遇到这类问题你就可以迎刃而解。

希望网友能够重视拼写问题。这个例子简单来说是老外说形式发票(proforma invoice,PI)的价格太高了,自己接受不了。网友用市场买菜那一套去还价,但比较可取的是,网友不是一上来就打个八折,而是坚决地否定了客户的减价要求,例子如下。

本叔,您好:

您的 BE 的一些表达其实不仅可以在一个案例中应用,而且可以灵活应用于其他背景中,真的可以体现一个业务员的说话水平。

下面是客户跟我在价格上纠结的一个例子。我报 5% 折扣梯度价格给客户,自己觉得已经写得很清楚了,但客户故意歪曲理解。我报样机价,然后根据数量逐步打折出一个阶梯价格,如下:

Sample

2～5 PCS   5% discount on sample
6～50 PCS   10% discount on sample
estimate shipping cost per PCS
99 USD/PCS   94.05 USD /PCS

89.10 USD /PCS   25 USD /PCS

客户回复的邮件如下。

Hello Mike,

I think I didn't understand your quotation, it is very different to the proforma invoice.

网友：我 PI 上的价格和报价是一样的，但是他非要截图给我说 PI 的应该是下面这样的。

I understood that the price for the sample would be 89.10 * 0.9 = 80.19 USD.

网友：他还把报价截图给我看，是我的报价格式模板有问题，还是客户不会算数，或是客户故意的？紧接着，他还给我分析了一下我们这个行业其他企业的价格和知名度，我报的价格他承受不起，没利润，卖不了……

Equivalent to Item 210B. When we take your price and convert to R$ including all import and local sales tax + margin we get R$ × ×.

The conclusion is that we can't pay for this.

In order to compete with the same sales conditions, our volume price would need to be × × USD.

网友：无论客户是不是故意的，我本着价格不能动的原则来解释，后面又说成本降不下来不能降价。以下是我的回复，麻烦您给优化一下。

As we discussed in the email, you are distributor in Brazil markets. So I didn't quote you the retail price,[1] please check: 540 USD is distributor sample price, then 2-5 pcs have a 5% off, 94.05 USD/pcs. 6-50 pcs have 10% off, 89.10 USD/unit, order above 6 pcs one time, there is 10% off, so the unit price will be 89.10 USD/unit.[2]

I totally understand your markets. High custom duties, high shipping cost, even over the value of some products.[3] We are factory, so we could provide you near machine cost step quotation.[4]

Right now, it is very tough for our factory, because we are factory, so many factory break down every month, every day for staff and

1. 有点离题了吧？人家在扯自己的利润不够，你却在扯没向他报零售价……"鸡同鸭讲"。
2. 我都看不下去了。有一个原则希望大家记住：当表达数据时，不要用BE。你需要的既不是华丽的英文，也不是简洁的英文。此时你需要的是表格！一个表格可以说明的事，不要用文字。如果真的不行，那就用两个表格。
3. 表达同理心，我理解你的苦处，这里赞一个！
4. 什么？near machine cost step quotation？我把每个词分开来译也没搞明白，我猜这是在说贴近生产成本吧，不过要表达这个说法，的确没有一个直接的字眼。

operating cost reason.

这一段网友是在叫苦。是啊,天天有工厂倒闭,天天有老板跳楼……但我不知道为什么要说这些,是为了解释上文的"为什么我能以贴近成本的便宜价位出售"吗?我希望不是,要不然就真的太可怜了。买两台设备就能打折,就能把底价报给客户……你让老外看了怎么想,这难道是传说中的以退为进策略?

We can give a lower price with this machine, use other "problem" spare parts assemble. But it is not our style, not conform our "quality is culture". Also, otherwise will be strongly effected by bad reputation.

这一段也很好玩。当年只要我一说贵,供应商(特别是香港和台湾地区,大陆的供应商会跳过这段废话,直接问目标价……)就会来一段以下说词:你要便宜的可以啊,我用料差点就行了。可是我们不会啊,为什么?因为我们跟人家不同啊,只有我们的是好东西啊,我没骗你,全世界都是坏人……当年,年少的我就是这样培养出对供应商的耐心的。是的,一分钱一分货绝对在理,但这一句很容易给人以上我说的那种感觉,你是不是高质量,客户心里自有数。

Purchasing season is coming, you are a wise boss. This machine model is our popular and featured products. So the machines (in stock and testing well) will be reserved very soon. Certainly, we can produce more, but the machine need to be tested about 7～14 days. it might be delay with your board.

这一小段反而不错。虽然用字不是特别好,却说出了:快点买,你需要入货,我有现货啊!这个号召行动(call for action)会有效果,BE 不需要优美的字,这样也就过关了。

Any requirements or doubt, don't hesitate to email.

Looking forward to your reply soon.

我觉得网友回复的这封邮件的中间部分先拿工厂说成本，后又拿产品说成本，有点乱，结尾也有点偏题。

作者的批评有以下几点。

1. 给不打折点个赞。不要一上来就给折扣，B2C 里意思一下减个零头是很常用的市井议价策略，但在 B2B 里就不要用这一套了。

2. 大方向对了，细节不好。写 BE 应该先把 B 理清，我感觉网友当时思想有点混乱……

3. 谈判方式太市井。我本想说有点中式，但其实更像那些江湖卖茶、卖保健品的感觉，都是那些"我用好料我怕谁""市道很差，你救救我吧，好人一生平安"的套路。不是说一定没用，只是我不会用而已。

纵观网友的布局，双方谈来谈去都还是在价钱这一个点上用力。你报阶梯价说的是价钱，他跟你扯没利润说的也是价钱。难道除了钱，你们之间已经没有火花了吗？据我所知，网友卖的产品是一种正在急速饱和的小型机器，行业产品的设计不太动脑，产品同质化开始严重。

就谈判技巧而言，既然价格不想退让，那就不要纠缠在这个点上，应该另开战线。

参考范文如下。

Hi,

　　Hope things go well with you.

　　I've discussed with my team regarding your target price, and you told me that you are comparing our product to your market competitor brand which we know quite well. They are supplied by another factory we know in China, and we are even from the same town. I have to say, we know their product inside out, and indeed we are not really competitive if price is your ONLY concern. In one word, their products are positioned as household toy while ours are tailored for professional sectors.

　　When you look closer to the features of the product, you can easily find out the differences:

　　Ⅰ. Longer product life - Our warranty is 3 years while they offer max 1 year. We start to see their performance going down after ×× times of operation.

　　Ⅱ. Casting material - Try it yourself. Plastic VS steel.

　　Ⅲ. Software - They accept only one input

这是整个策略的重点：不要在互不相让的价钱上纠缠不清，明智的做法是另开战线跟他扯一扯其他的，例如功能。在开始洽谈的阶段我不赞成扯品质，因为这不是客户很直观就能明白的。这就正如 Luxor 从来不扯巧克力的口味一样。我们侧重的是颜值，功能跟颜值都是很直观的。

file type while we support a range of different inputting files. We invest quite some resources to develop a user-friendly SW.

Ⅳ. Size - Our machine can make models 2 times of their max - size. A key significant difference in our market.

So, although we are all called "3D printing machine", the application range defines[1] the cost and hence the selling price. Of course, if you are looking for toy, they could be a better option.[2]

However, if you are not targeting that highly price-sensitive market, our machine could reward you with much better profit.[3] We pride ourselves with our technology. Not too many companies in this industry could be considered as real a competitor of us.[4]

"Back to school" season is coming in Sept and education sector will start their purchasing plan soon.[5] You will be able to hit this wave if you make your decision soon enough. Many of our customers have already placed order last month. I am looking forward to hearing from you.

以上是我编的，业内人士别认真，我只是为了举例。

1. "define" 是个实用的字。
2. 这是个险招。万一人家真的想买玩具呢？若真是这样也罢，不是你的，永远都不属于你。
3. 此处的潜台词是："你就去跟人家斗价呗！你去呀，怎么不去呀？"
4. 要不要这样说，看你的底气了……
5. 此处的潜台词是："连怎样做生意我都教你了。机不可失，我们聪明的客户都已经下单了，你却还在跟我扯那一块几毛钱。"

Regards,
Ben

> **本部分建议掌握的 BE 金句**
>
> 1. If you are not targeting highly price-sensitive market, our product could reward you with much better profit.
> 2. We pride ourselves with...

因为原材料涨价我也要涨了,该怎么写

朋友圈的外贸人都在感叹原材料越来越贵,而此时我却要来一个主动加价的例子。回想一下,过去大部分的 BE 好像都是被动的——老外来一封信,我们回一封信,见招拆招,这次我们主动点。你的原材料供应商加价时都是很主动的,你有什么理由不主动?

我访问了一下受原材料价格上涨影响的外贸人,他们大致都说是行业供求在整固中,很多金属和物料都供不应求了。要是这是一个事实,那么这个问题就不会是一个短期的问题,而是中长期的,所谓结构性的问题,那就更需要转嫁给客户了。

有人会问:全行业都知道原材料贵了,我还用说什么理由吗?这是个心态问题,就算客户心知肚明,供应商还是有责任把事情的全局

表达清楚。你比客户更了解供应链的任何改变，也有责任评估改变给客户带来的影响，把影响减至最低。

本叔在这里为大家科普一下，加插一些关于成本浮动的知识。一般来说，原材料和外汇是两个最常见的理由，而这两者之间，大概又有一定的关系，最直接的是，在沙特和其他产油国没有人为增产的情况下，美元向下，石油向上，你的原材料就会涨价（塑料的原材料是石油，至于五金，我也无法理解，但很多时候都是一起升的）。美元向下，相对来说人民币就会向上，你的成本也就高了（毕竟你的老板不是给你发美元而是人民币）。材料贵了，人力成本又高了，那么美元向下对外贸是个大打击——当你用美元报价，收老外美元的时候。

美元为什么会跌？这是一个十分人为的操作（对，一直指控中国操纵人民币的美国，自己有一个叫联储局的组织，它其中一项工作是决定美元走向）。2008年金融危机后，美元靠大规模减息降美元资产（更重要的是负债……），不过这是BE，不是经济学课，就不说太多了。

除了货币相关的成本浮动，另一种原因是供求问题。十几年前人人都说工厂好做，订单多到接不过来。然后，这些低增值的OEM加工厂就如雨后春笋一样冒出来。在长三角和珠三角，几个工人跑出来，众筹一两台加工机器，这就开了一家工厂。再然后，工厂太多，供过于求。最后，一批批实力不够的工厂倒闭了，行业洗牌了（我们叫供应链整固）。留下来的工厂痛定思痛，大家就可能有意无意地有了默契，"赚不够，就不做了"。就这样一层堆一层，物料价格便高涨了。

怎么破解？这不是你我能破解的。要知道，特别是原材料，这些"剩者为王"的企业都是相当有实力的。如果只靠市场，有可能十年之后才能有幸看到转变。

好了，以上是给大家一个宏观的概念。我们现在回到 BE 的话题。以下是我编的例子。

Hi James,

Hope things are going well with you.

In the last few months we have been trying to manage the situation. Now it seems to be out of our control and we have to make this communication with you on the situation regarding the upward trend of material cost and our corresponding plan.[1]

Material has been up by 15% and it is said to be a structural change-meaning: the upward trend is not going to cease in a short period of time.[2] Our supplier told us it is the raw material processor who has monopolized the supply chain that started the price-up, affecting all the industries related to plastic. We have checked with more than 3 suppliers and they all shared the same answer.[3] We believe this is a situation we have no options

1. 开场白，说一下自己不是没想过解决问题（主观能动性到位），而是因为该问题实在不是我能控制的（客观不可抗）。

2. 15% 不是个小数目，而且还是一个中长期的趋势——先把事实的负面影响说在前头。要简单，抓要点！

3. 表明价格上涨的原因是我方核实过的，千真万确！

but to face.

We have investigated how to dilute[1] the impact on our customers and 2 suggestions have come out. Here it is:

Ⅰ. As per our negotiation with the supplier, any order before end of Dec. could maintain the old price. Therefore, we suggest a one-time bulk (with pre-paid deposit) order from you to reduce the amount of affected qty. We suggest ×× PCS which matchs your qty of last 6 months.[2]

Ⅱ. We suggest you put forward an annual order forecast so that we could negotiate our consolidate demand with suppliers and try to combat with the increase. Volume is always the best way for a cost down.[3]

I strongly recommend we start to take action immediately. New quotation (as attached) will be effected by Jan with around 10% of increase. About 70%[4] of our cost derives from the material and the impact is too heavy for us to suffer. We have no choices but to raise the price. I hope this is understandable to you.

1. "dilute"表示稀释。这是个物理学的名词，但在这里完美地借用来说明我方尽力帮客户把不良影响稀释一下。
2. 这个思路很重要。要是一上来你就告诉买家昨天下的单要加价了，99%的买家会不高兴。但你给出一个过渡期，买家还有时间准备，这才叫合作，这才叫服务。这样做你还能收到一张大单！
3. 这是一个好习惯——做预测，很多人都没有做。你可以利用加价这个机会，让自己知道将来的订单有多少。
4. 这个要小心，千万不要前言不对后语。70%要确保一致性，而不是时而80%，时而60%。物料上涨15%，我才给你涨10%，企业良心了。另外千万记住，你没有责任在当中承担任何的涨幅风险。这是你做 OEM 的权利，不要被老外一句"not fair"之类的废话骗了！

本部分建议掌握的 BE 金句（此文通篇都是精华）

1. Material has been up by 15% and it is said to be a structural change.
2. We have investigated how to dilute the impact on our customers and two suggestions have come out.
3. We believe this is a situation we have no options but to face.
4. Therefore, we suggest a one-time bulk（with pre-paid deposit）order from you to reduce the amount of affected qty.
5. We suggest you put forward an annual order forecast so that we could negotiate our consolidate demand with suppliers and try to combat with the increase.
6. Volume is always the best way for a cost down.
7. About 70% of our cost derives from the material and the impact is too heavy for us to suffer. We have no choices but to raise the price. I hope this is understandable to you.

有没有遇到过客户拿着几年前的报价单来跟你下单

你有没有遇到过客户拿着几年前的报价单来跟你下单？

你知不知道有多少报价单没有写"有效期"？有效期是很多报价单都漏掉的东西，就算没漏，也有不少是瞎写的，只有到出事时，才后悔没思考这个日期。

那么怎么定呢？这个问题就回到了"价格为什么会变"这个问题上。成本是影响价格的其中一个（但不是唯一的）因素。成本变动因素包括原材料、外汇汇率等。作为供应商，即使再笨你应该也不会报一个10年有效期的价钱吧？当然，行业不同，报价有效期也不一样。油价变动大，原材料商只会给你报一个很短（可能是几天）的有效期。作为中间商，你应该特别小心地跟工厂沟通有效期，不然你夹在中间，容易赔了夫人又折兵。

下面的例子就是这个问题。一年前旧的报价却被客户拿来压价，网友怀疑老外是否改了上面的数字。世界之大，无奇不有，这样的可能性是存在的。但不管他怎么弄，最后决定以什么价格卖给他的人，是你。你绝对可以一笑置之，何必生气。来，我们看看例子。

这个客户没有实质性的邮件文案，整个事件发生的时间有点长，我就长话短说了。

2015年的时候有个新客户来访，当时我的实习期还没有满，老板和我一起接待，客户是有备而来，当场买了样品，很低很低的价格,这个价格是老板在接待洽谈的过程中给的,也是客户亲手把现金递给老板的。

在洽谈时,我拿了一份产品目录册给客户,客户选中三款产品,并在这三款产品旁边标注了价格,我自己也备份了一份。

但是客户回国后,测试样品没问题,要买大货,已是2016年,而且他们拍照给我看的当时的目录册上标记的价格,和我备份的不一样!

我没有问客户是不是故意改了,我说现在的价格有更新,价格也是有有效期的,会重新发一份新的报价给他。更重要的是老板和我说绝对不能再以之前的那个样品价格卖了,那个是完全没有利润的,新的报价比之前的高了很多。

客户就在Skype上发表了意见:这是去年你说的价格,怎么我买大货比买样货还贵呢?你这产品价格再怎么更新,价格要高这么多吗?当我不懂行啊。

然后我就给客户发了一封挑战性邮件。

Hello C,

Kindly find below words about price:

For items quote last year is the sample EXW price in CKD condition instead of finished one.

We never quote price below ×× USD in finished condition to customer from any countries.

简单一个"never",斩钉截铁、清楚明确。这就是BE思维。

For item PSA, you can check the upgraded characteristics from the picture. It worthy.

这里"characteristics"是不是该用"feature"？这一点我不完全肯定，要看升级了的是什么。如果你去查字典，两个字的字面意义很接近，但用法上又有一点区别。不过，这也是看你的客户是什么语系的。美国人和欧洲人对这些细微的差别会有一点点不同的理解。这只是其中一个例子。另外，要表达物有所值，"It worthy"用法是不正确的，正确的搭配应该是"It is worthy of it"，但大部分欧美人都用"worth"这个词，"It is worth it"，这也是惯例吧。

We are lose money here on your request price, how can we provide quality printer with best service for you?

这句话的修辞可以更好，但现在也是一个合格的表达。"lose"改为"losing"。

Either the quote or PI have a valid date, right? That's why I requote here.

用得很奇怪，但还是知道你想说什么。

Don't you think we can not making profit from this price?

好了，你有点太激动了，要知道，冷静是有威慑力的。

We are one professional manufacturer, cost is clear to customer as listed.

We do not want negotiate on price much as we have pricing rule accordingly to customer's ability.

哇！过了！比本叔还霸气。"customer's ability"？是不是大客报贵点小客报便宜点？这一点我想你是错了。不过，"we do not want to negotiate on price"是一个可以用的句子，我见到不少老外这样用，不会显得没礼貌。不卑不亢是一个不易把握的度，看到这里网友的言辞开始有点激进了。

As I was told that our product can solve some problem easily there, which means our equipment can save your cost to some extend.

这个好。我在前面说过不要在价格上纠缠，而是另开战线。这里就对了，"solve some problem easily"虽写得不实在（some 是什么），但和"save your cost to some extend"一起就把那个价值写了出来。你可能会觉得这没什么大不了，全行业都一样。但你要明白，写出来跟不写出来，本身就是个很大的区别！

Personally, I will do all I can do to help you solve the price problem. Even not ask sales commissions of this order, and convert to discount to you.

这里写得不好。你有没有拿提成这回事跟买家没关系。老外看了以后的内心戏肯定是："你是想我可怜你吗？"

How about it?

你想问什么？表述不清！

Anyway, we are looking forward creating a partnership and cooperation between A co. and B co. here.

Yours sincerely,

J

不知道客户有没有看邮件，但是他在 Skype 上找我了，现在我和客户的关系维持得还行，有新的产品我还会发给他们看。回头来看看，是不是因为这个文案太青涩了，客户都懒得回复？烦请本叔帮忙用地道的 BE 润色一下，感激不尽！

作者点评：原文有点太情绪化了，请相信，冷静是一种力量。参考范文如下。

Hi,

Thanks for your "re-enquiry". I hope everything is fine with you and thanks for the re-connection.[1]

However, the price you indicated is not valid. That was a price of a modulus（Note: not a finished product）quoted 2 years ago, so the value of modulus is obviously not equivalent to that of finished product. We never offer finished goods at this price.[2]

As a matter of fact, the latest product has many upgraded features compared to the one you've seen. The improvement aims for higher operation efficiency which in turn will save your daily costs. Many of our customers appreciate the change and it is proven to be welcomed by the market. I am sure your investment is worth it.[3]

I have attached a table of comparison between the old and new version so you know what you are paying for.[4] High frequency

1. 礼貌不要丢！

2. 清楚解释那只是个误会。至于是不是真的是误会，那就只有你知道了。

3. 其实，大部分机械供应商都应该重视这一点。你的客户购买设备不是用来玩的，而是把设备当作生财工具。工具的价值在于它的产出，这才是客户眼中的价值！

4. 正如我之前说过的，有很多时候BE不一定是良方。一个表格比一堆英文更清晰、更明白。

user will find aggressive cost reduction[1] by operating our new model machine. We also provide full after-sales service so be assured that you are well supported.[2]

Looking forward to work with you.

Regards,

Ben

1. "aggressive"不仅可以用在一个人的性格上，也可以用在节约成本这码事上，也可以说是开车的风格等。
2. 这不是所有对手都有的服务，所以我们值得提。但就算是全行业都有的服务，我们也得提。提与不提，本身就是个很大的区别。

后记：网友告诉我客户最终还是下单了。即使这样还是要注意客户是否在心理埋下了一粒种子，一有机会就换掉你。拿到订单后，我们一定要好好提供专业服务，这才是长治久安之策。

本部分建议掌握的 BE 金句

1. The improvement aims for ×× which in turn will save your daily costs.

2. I have attached a table of comparison between ×× and ×× so you know what you are paying for.

**REALLY GOOD NEWS
YOU WANT TO EXPAND YOUR MARKET**

第 2 章 分 销

BE 不在于华丽的英文语句，而在于到位的沟通，思维在语言之上。

这一章讲的是分销。本章第二部分的案例是"总有老外想与我合作",老外很有诚意想与你合作,但你思想保守,坚持认为利润空间不大就不卖。这个例子讲的就是个分销的苗芽,这个苗芽能不能壮大就看你怎么处理这段关系了。

有些网友做得不错,客户看上了他的产品,并想包销在地区市场上做独家。本章第一部分就是这样的例子,可惜网友的英文表达不到位,把本来一件美事表达成"你不……我就不跟你玩"之类的,并不像在谈生意。我听到不少老外抱怨说他们对中国商人的感觉是唯利是图。这是废话中的废话,言不及利,难道还要跟你说好做彼此的天使吗?但老外之所以这样说,我看很多时候问题是出在表达上。

BE 就是你的气质。

如何应对包销

同一件事,同一个立场,用不同的写法表达出来的效果就会完全不同。这个道理你可以在这一部分的例子中体会到。全篇英文表达到位,唯独给人的感觉不是在聊生意,而是在谈判。你会问:叔,人生不就是一场又一场的谈判吗?叔只能苦笑:谈判是不是意味着大家要穿上西装正儿八经地聚集在会议室里讨论,那种才叫谈判吗?其实绝大部分决策都是在谈笑风生中成型的。这种气氛是要靠业务员去营造的。好的 BE 就能做到这一点。

以下是这例子的背景。

1. 一款产品开发出来,公司花费了差不多50万元,一年只开发1～2款。

2. 一个业务员将这款产品推荐给合作多年的马来西亚老客户(这个老客户也是这个业务员当年辛辛苦苦从竞争对手那里抢回来的,一年采购数量1000),接着客户在市场上发现另外一个人(这个是后面开发的新客户)也在卖这个产品,一年采购数量1500。

3. 跟进这个老客户的业务员此时已更换成另外一个业务员,老客户要求谈包销,新业务的回复如下。

Dear AAA,

May I ask your annual demand for each model if it is the exclusive model in your market?

一上来就问付得起多少钱,本叔我卖巧克力都不敢这么做。

Please let me explain the exclusivity in our company as following:

不错,用"let me explain"让人舒服。这里用"exclusivity policy"会比较好,让人感觉我们是一视同仁的。

(1) The tooling cost for each model is around ××,×× USD.

(2) The certificate cost for each model is around ××,×× USD.

(3) It will take at least 8 months to finish one new BPM model, the development cost is ××,×× USD.

Totally, it will cost ××,×× USD for one model, please kindly understand that we need to keep the balance between investment and output (orders).

Based on the very large cost on one NEW BPM model, Normally, we will not sign the exclusivity with customers, there are two solutions for the product conflict:

(1) For the models you selected, please tell us the annual demand and we will check if it is possible to keep you as the only distributor in your market.

不是"only distributor",而是"sole agency/ sole distributor"。

(2) If the annual demand is small, we will suggest to make the product colour different for avoiding the conflict.

我看到你在提供其他方案了,这一点没错。

So far, the orders from BBB is more than yours,[1] so it is very hard to make the decision, however, we respect our relationship,[2] any more suggestion, please feel free to tell us and let's discuss about it.[3]

Best regards,

××

1. 这里你是在说:AAA 你算老几?
2. 啊,你是想让客户感激你吗,我听起来觉得很让人反感。
3. 这句就像在说"老外你可有可无"。

整体来说,这篇 BE 写得还可以。我一直强调,BE 不在于华丽的英文语句,而在于到位的沟通,思维在语言之上。这一篇算是达到这个标准了,只是语气太强硬,想必你对多年的朋友绝不会如此吧。所以,这一篇的问题在于不恰当的英语表达。

我听不少老外说过,他们对中国商人的感觉是唯利是图。说真的,这是废话中的废话，难道要跟你说好做彼此的天使吗？但老外之所以这样说，我看很多时候问题是出在表达上。这一篇就大概有点这个意味了，一个辛苦争取来的合作多年的伙伴受到冷淡对待的故事。当然，我知道你们的本意并非如此，那不如让我们看看原文要怎样修改会比较好。

Hi AAA,

  First of all I would like to appreciate your intention to work exclusively with us. This means to me our product can serve your market well and I assume that also means you are happy with our relationship.[1] Look back on our long successful history it makes perfect sense that we can work further and closer together.[2]

  Yet, the adoption of exclusivity could be a direct financial hit to our business. Here I list out my concerns:

  Ⅰ. ROI: Considerable investment[3] on our NPI[4] process: designing, tooling, certification, timing... If you are interested I can send you a breakdown to give you a better idea.

1. 这是个事实，我的产品能帮你挣钱，我们都应该很高兴。
2. 回顾一下，对双方历史性的合作做出高度认同。
3. "Considerable"是个得体的字眼，它没说我们投入了多少，但也不表示我们的投入太少，意思是总体数额还是值得重视的。
4. new product introduction，新产品开发流程。

II. Put yourself into my shoes,[1] I wish you could understand where I come from. I need to go volume[2] in order to amortize[3] my cost.

III. As a result, I would be more than happy[4] to discuss with anyone about exclusivity[5] with a contracted volume.[6] Only in this way could I focus on my role as a manufacturer while partnering with someone like you as local market experts on sales.[7]

IV. Having said that, other factors like branding effort, channel coverage...could also be of consideration.

1. 可以译为"将心比心",很好用,常用来说服客户。
2. 很巧,"走量"的英语表达是"go volume"。这不是中式英文。
3. "amortize"是"分摊"的意思。模具之类的固定成本要分摊到单件上,就用这个词。
4. 这里表达十分快乐的意思。
5. 独家经营。
6. 这里也表达了我们的独家经营是要签协议的,客户要接受合同对产出价值的约束,而不是随便说说。
7. 我们就这样分工吧!我专心生产,你专心销售!

I am open for discussion if above sound reasonable to you.¹ Meanwhile, I believe exclusivity is NOT the only way to serve our best interest.² There must be some more opportunities out there.

Thanks for your trust in our business. We will keep talking.

Regards,

Ben

---

1. "你若是听起来合理"，这句翻译成中文绝对很奇怪。这世上既然有中式英文，那有西式中文也说得过去。我想说的是，世上的语言都有自己背后的逻辑，而这些逻辑又跟各自的文化历史有关，所以勉强拉在一起就会让人觉得很奇怪。

2. "其实我们不想跟你谈独家"的会聊天版本。不把话说死，我们除了聊独家还有很多可以聊的。用对的话术，就能把这些意思表达得有技巧。

本部分建议掌握的 BE 金句（如何婉拒包销）

1. The adoption of exclusivity could be a direct financial hit to our business. Here I list out my concerns.

2. Put yourself into my shoes.

3. I need to go volume in order to amortize my cost.

4. I believe exclusivity is NOT the only way to serve our best interest.

总有老外想与我合作

什么生意才需要代理呢？一直以来总有人问我如何成为 Luxor 的代理，而我一般都礼貌地回绝。不是因为我高傲，而是目前我们的产品不太适合。那为什么不适合呢？我们可以先想一想，为什么我们需要代理，为什么好好的自己不去做，非要找个中间人？

目前电子商务的发展太迅速了，很多人都忘记了甚至不知道十多年前生意是怎样做的。代理的存在是有其合理性的。

1. 他比你懂他的市场。最简单的例子是海外市场。

2. 他的资源很适合。对我来说，婚庆公司便是这类。

3. 他能让产品增值。这个增值的定义很广泛，举例说：

（1）你每次出货只收现金，出货前付清；他却可以接受给客户提供两三个月的账期。

（2）他帮你存货。你每次一柜一柜地卖，他却可以一件一件地卖给客户（B2B 和 B2C 的分别）。

（3）他能为当地客户提供必要的售后服务，而你自己是做不了的。

例子还有很多，但我也不是分销的专家，就只能写到这里。下面这个案例是有个老外找到网友，提出诸多要求（要求之一就是做代理），我们来看看网友是如何回复的。

Dear Ben:

看完您的 BE，我觉得我写的英文邮件都不能看，我把客户和我的全部往来邮件都发给您，您帮忙看一下怎么回复客户比较合适，谢谢！

事情是这样的，客户第一封邮件就直接针对我们具体的某一个产品询价，说明他是知道我们公司的，所以在第一封邮件里面我就直接报价给他，没有拖沓。

在第二封邮件里客户说了他的三点顾虑和担忧。

第一，客户是澳大利亚的，他想要我们其他澳大利亚客户的电话和信息，他想打电话过去了解情况，我说其他客户不愿意这样，就没有给他。

第二，客户说价格高，我说刚开始做你需要用好的设备。

第三，客户问我们设备核心部件的参数，我告诉他我们用的都是西门子这样的大品牌，他很满意。

第三封邮件他就说到了我们的设备在澳大利亚没有售后，针对这一点他想做我们的代理，帮助我们开发澳大利亚的客户，并再一次说到了我们的价格高，想让我们给他一个样机，但是价格要实实在在便宜。然后再次说要澳大利亚使用过我们设备的客户的信息，让他打电话。

基本上邮件内容就这么多，我也不知道哪个是突破口，怎样回复他。

第一封信是老外发来的，是这样：

Thank you J. I am still considering.

1. I need to be able to speak to an existing customer of yours who is using the machine in Australia—pls provide a name/phone number.

2. I need a cheaper machine—US $×× is too high for us as a start

up; do you have another model or a demo unit?

3. Pls provide details of the flow meter and pump the machine uses?

4. Who are your service/warranty agents in Australia?

regards,

N

这是一个上好的 BE——简单、要点明确、清晰。

(注：此文出自老外。)

下一篇是网友的回复。

Dear N,

Ⅰ. We are sorry to say that we cloud not provide you customer name and phone number, from your side[1] we think that you want to know more about our filling machine from Australia.[2] But dear N, CE certificate could help you to understand the quality of our BIB filling machine, and we had some working video of BIB single head filling machine for your check.[3]

1. 又是"your side"，"您那边"，100%的中式英文！

2. "我猜你是想知道"，好复杂的句式，这是有多少内心戏……

3. 这个要点是可以的，有证书又有视频，就算没有样板也可以初步解决老外对产品质量的信任问题了。客户要求提供证明在国外很普遍，LinkedIn 在开始时也有这个推荐的功能。可是这不代表你一定要答应，万一他是竞争对手呢。

Ⅱ. Dear N,[1] a reliable supplier and stable working performance filling machine is very important for you as a start, you need not spend more time on production capacity and filling volume accuracy from your email we get that you know our company manufacturing 10 years BIB filling machine in this field. We do not have any cheaper filling machine recommend to you.[2]

Ⅲ. Flowmeter we are using are YYY from German magnetic flowmeter, specification as following:

PLC we are using are Siemens from German. (there are too many information, could you specific which part you want to know?)

Pump we suggest you purchase 3 kw centrifugal pump.

Ⅳ. Dear N, we do not have service agents in Australia, on one side is[3] we just start Australia market for 2 years, the sales volume could not support us to start an agent in Australia. On the other hand our filling machine has few after sales problem, seals ring abrasion is customers frequency questions, but they can

1. 左一句"dear"右一句"dear"，你们的关系真的很好吗？
2. 网友的逻辑是："老外你别贪便宜，便宜没好货，我们都卖了10年了，只有这些产品，没有便宜货。"这是一个专业的判断。人家看来也是个懂行的，他是不是真的需要一台又贵又好的机器起步，这一点我不知道他会怎么想。我只能跟你说，每次我说供应商的价格贵，80%的回复都是条件反射似地说"对啊，因为我们的产品都是好东西"。你此番表述可能是出于好意，但对方会有什么样的反应，这很难说。
3. "on one side"你是想说"一方面"吧？不能这样用！正确的用法是"on the one hand"。

replace it by themselves under our instruction.[1]

All in all, people always saying seeing is believing, if you have time, welcome to visit our factory and you will know which kind of supplier you are going to choose. Please see attachment.

If you have any other query or problems, we would love to provide you our suggestions.

Regards,

J

1. 这两个理由也是合理和充分的，看到这里我想说"在一起，在一起"了。这个澳大利亚人能提供的，正是你欠缺的！这个销量你也不用太在意，国外的消费习惯是要有售后服务，如果你总是没有的话，产品发展也会被限制。这就类似于先有鸡还是先有蛋的问题，有人愿意这样做，又不花你的钱，你为什么不做呢？估计你想说眼见为实，有图有真相，可是老外的语言里是没有这种表达的，所以他很难理解你。我记得我在老外老板面前说过"work like a donkey"，她就一脸疑惑。

这封回信在 E（English）上还有很多改善空间，但 B（business）的思维就算不错了。我们再看看下面的回复。

Thank you for your response and all the detailed information, J

Your machine looks very impressive and the parts are very good brands.

I appreciate that you do not have sufficient sales in Australia of your machine ×× or similar machine to give me a customer reference I can contact or a machine I can see working?

老外这一段的句式有些奇怪，但我们还是可以猜到一个大概意思。再者，只有中国人那么在乎语言的文法。

On top of that you have no after sales support in Australia if anything goes wrong—nothing is 100% perfect with machinery... not even a BMW or Mercedes!

This is a very major and unacceptable risk and unknown for a small business like mine to carry.

I am happy and willing to help promote your machine in Australia and have your future customers come and visit my winery site in Brisbane to see it working as well as help your sales on the phone to other local customers.

But I cannot afford your machine at US $×× shipping + import duty + local GST + cost of pump etc. or all the risks above.

My offer is that you send me a demo machine at a very substantial discount—including shipping and I will buy a pump here...

In return I will help you sell more of the machine in Australia and NZ and be a little like your local agent...

I have a very good knowledge of local prices and the competitor ×× machines and prices from Europe and US and can help customers understand and appreciate how good your ×× machines are in quality and maybe price to the competition.

Please consider further.

Regards,

N

老外这封回信有情有理。有一点可以肯定，他很感兴趣，并且正在努力游说网友。这绝对是一件好事。

我对这样的合作非常支持。因此我的回复会比较积极。以下是参考范文。

Hi N,

First of all, I appreciate your willingness to distribute our product in your market. That is extremely encouraging as I see it as your positive feedback on our product and its opportunity in your market.[1] For me, starting a new agency in a new country is a matter of chicken and egg — on the one hand, we do not have enough business resources to support an agency; on the other hand, we need a solid after-sales infrastructure to take in more business. It looks like we have business to discuss.[2]

Regarding your request for contacting our

1. 老手段，一开始要赞美。这是一个很科学的沟通方式。
2. 这又是一个拉近距离的技巧，叫作坦白。大方地说出自己对国外代理的看法和担忧，这样一来直达本文的核心问题，也能真正地拉近沟通距离。"infrastructure"这个词有点深，但是很500强。最后一句"looks like we have business to discuss"打开了对话的大门，气氛很好。

existing customers for reference—the fact is that we are unable to do it due to 2 reasons.

  First, most of our customer require privacy and some have even signed with us a NDA.[1] Second, to be honest, we have no clue how good/bad they would comment on our machine. As I stated above, we are weak in local after sales service.[2]

1. 不要回避问题，他已经两次提出要跟你的客户联络。但我们是铁了心不让步，上文中网友已经直接说了"不"，这次把理由再说一回。这个产品是否真的会签NDA（non-disclosure agreement，保密协议）我不清楚，但如果合理的话，这个理由就很强大。一般对方也不会再追问了。为什么？因为现在你要是能违反你和客户的NDA让我联络，是不是将来有一天他也会被你出卖？这个思维，做OEM的读者要好好想想，不要总主动把你跟某某客户的产品随便放在展厅。

2. 这是一个险招，也不是很有必要写。我看你是吃定他了，那么直说我们担心的事也不是坏事，跟上文能对接好。要不要写就看你自己了。

To lower your risk, let's discuss on your proposal regarding the demo machine. We could offer a set of machine, with all the necessary parts and tool kit at about $××—a price that we have never offered before.[1] What we expect, in return, is to have an exclusive demo workshop in your location so that we could forward all of our local inquries to you and suggest them visit your site.[2] We are also keen on[3] seeing a plan from you as how you are going to promote the product locally. Let's put it in written form and I am sure our discount is worth of your time to put it in place.[4]

Besides, I am curious why you are knowledgeable to this specific machine. Is that anything to do with your winery?

Let's keep talking.

Regards,
Ben

1. 我个人认为，这样是非常合理的。当然，你的样机他也一定会自用，但如果这样能带来更多的生意，那这个折扣也只是个投资。关键还是看你怎么利用他帮你做更多事。
2. 你不想名片上多一个澳大利亚的地址吗？独家啊！
3. "be keen on" 用来表达对某事很感兴趣。一个简单但又不常用的词组。
4. 这里的潜台词是：我要与你合作了，你去写写计划要怎么做这个市场吧。既然老外你那么想做我们的代理，我又很有诚意地给你减价了，那你得对我负责，做点功课吧。
这个你真的有必要知道。既然他说自己"know very well about the machine"，那总得有个原因吧，他是不是在吹牛，看看他的回答便可知一二。

总的来说，这里教的是真遇到合适的代理时，你要怎么去谈。有老外说要做代理，你不要太兴奋，也不要不懂得把握机会。BE 的应用在谈判当中扮演了一个很关键的角色。

REALLY GOOD NEWS
YOU WANT TO EXPAND YOUR MARKET

第 3 章　品　　质

品质的重点是在一个合理设计的生产流程下，反复在流程中检测错误，就算最笨的工人也没有办法把事情搞砸，这才叫"品质生产"！品质，靠的不是工匠精神，也不是老板和工人的良心，靠的只有一个：流程！

另一个需要大篇幅介绍的要点，是质量问题的沟通。

在 B2B 中，因为质量问题导致客户扣款不付、不收货，乃至退货等都十分常见，怎么办？首先，你自身必须过硬，拥有一个真正的质量应变能力（B）。其次，在这个前提之下，才是你去沟通这方面问题的能力。品管有不少专业用语（E），就算是一个地道的老外也不一定懂。这个可参考本章第四部分。如果遇到被扣款不付的情况要如何应对？看看本章第一部分和第二部分中的连环例子，你可能会有点头绪。

很多人抱怨客户只想跟工厂打交道，这不是没有原因的。一固然是价钱，二是他质疑你在生产工厂那边是否真的有话语权。本章第三部分中原文的回复容易让人觉得你只是个无决策权的中介。当发生问题，在责任方尚不明确时，你别急着道歉，态度要积极，不卑不亢，先说明要多了解情况。B2B 的客户和供应商双方是在合作，所以客户有责任提供足够信息配合你查找出原因。

客户由于质量问题不付款怎么办（1）

接下来要讲的这个例子是一个有关验货/付款的拉锯战，相当典型。故事很长，我把它分成了两部分。

我直接引用了网友提供的背景，删去了商业机密。

TCJ 款式为其中一个款式，此款因为中间沟通的问题，导致标准模糊，最终造成大货部分货品外观/尺寸不是很好。客户是中间商，却以最终客户投诉为由要求扣除公司总货款的20%。在公司同意的情况下，剩余的货款仍然拖至6月末付。此时公司还有客户最后一批货物TCS。TCS第一次尾查并没有通过，于是我们就安排了最终客户指定的第三方（简称Q）验货，在拿到通过的验货报告后，我们要求中间商客户付清前一笔货款。

以下是网友发的邮件，在这里希望大家记住，拼写检查必须做。

Dear all,

　　TCS already passed the final inspection issued by Q. So from our side,[1] we don't think it's necessary for tomorrow's re-inspection.[2]

1. 这句话很中式，你可能想说"我们这边认为"，建议改为"from our point of view"，想霸气点可以用"in my view"，将"view"变作动词就更霸气。不过，你是在做生意，不是在演戏，不用太霸气。

2. 整段话还是不错的，把自己的看法直接、清晰地表达出来了。

But pls clearly to be noted,[1] indicated by our company's policy we must receive at least 50% payment for TCJ no later than Monday,[2] no shipment will be allowed to arrange for TCS before we received any serious official[3] payment confirmation.

I am sorry for this, but I need to follow company's policy. And pls let me know your action ASAP.

Thanks & Best regards,

Ms. D（网友的简称。）

参考范文如下。

Hi all,[4]

Following the positive inspection result from Q, I don't see the need of re-inspection. Quality should be well accepted according to our defined process.[5] As a separate issue,[6] may I remind you that we must receive 50% of the payment before we can proceed with your shipment? I am not able to release anything without a solid[7] proof. Please help me to help

1. 这句是常错的。首先，讲一点文法："but"永远不用来开句。这里应该用"however"来代替"but"。其次，句式太复杂，"pls be clearly noted that"会好一点，但只是好一点点……
2. 此处该有连接词吧，有点奇怪。
3. "official"就够了，你可能在类似的场合见过有人用"serious"，但用在这里不对。
4. 我知道你们以前学的都是"DEAR××"。跟所有人都用"DEAR"，你们难道不觉得不对劲吗？
5. 多用"process"。在品管领域，"process"是圣旨。既有process而不follow，死罪。
6. 这的确是两码事。
7. "solid"这个词很好用。

you with an in-time delivery.[1]

I am sorry, but a rule is a rule.[2] Thanks for your understanding.

Regards,
Ben

1. 这句不得了，潜台词是：我已尽力了，你得自己争气啊……
2. 第一句可以不要，语气有点生硬，用不用就看你跟客户的关系了。

接下来是客户三个不同部门的同事围攻网友 D 小姐。

第一个：

Hi Dora,

We had already advised that there was no need to arrange Q inspection but let our QC Janny to do the re-final inspection. Please confirm that you had already sorted out all the problems as what our QC Janny found on her final inspection. Her previous final inspection was rejected with a lot of issues. Please reply.

Regard,
A

第二个：

Hi Carmen, Janny needs to do this reinspection and eyeball the whole stock.

"eyeball" 这个词很常见，也很有现场监督验收的画面感，值得大家学习。

Regards,
B

第三个：

I agree with B.

We need to ensure the workmanship issues have truly been addressed.

这句是很典型的废话，500强常见。

Regards,

C

本部分建议掌握的 BE 金句

1. Following ... I do not see the need of ...
2. Quality should be well accepted according to our defined process.
3. As a separate issue, may I remind you that...
4. Please help me to help you with an in-time delivery.

客户由于质量问题不付款怎么办（2）

续上一个例子，双方一直在拉锯是先重新验货还是先付钱。这里跳过一些细节，后来老外翻脸了，直指 D 小姐办事不力，并向她的老板 K 先生投诉。这个例子中的 BE 都写得很专业，所以就不多做修改了，那么我们就静观事情的发展。

1. 下面这封邮件是老外发给 K 和 D 的。

Hi K/D,

I tried to call D's phone but failed.

We relooked into the remittance of USD×× and found that we had accidently paid you too much. We had now stopped the payment to recalculate. We will send through payment again after recalculation. I wanted to discuss with Dora on the phone but it seems that you are avoiding answering my phone calls.

老外一直在强调，是 D 不接电话。先不管 D 不接电话是否属实，我想说这是一个 500 强常用的把戏：目的是让看到这封邮件的人对 D 的印象不好，谁对谁错我不知道，但他这么一说，D 就好像很不专业。作为 500 强的老油条，我一看到这句话就会多一个心眼。

We do not know what reason you could not arrange our QC's inspection. There must be some quality issues otherwise you could have arranged our QC to check the goods. We made 30% upfront payment on this product based on the trust to your company. It is unfair that you do not follow our instruction. As my discussion with my boss, we would rather not deliver the skirts if there is going to have potential problem.

依我看，不让他们重新验货这件事也没那么容易。

You must communicate with us ASAP as tomorrow is the cutoff date for the skirts!

Regards

2. 下面这封邮件是老外的高层追加的。

K,

I would appreciate a phone call from you as dealing with Dora on this matter has not been beneficial for either of us.

这一句有时可以害惨一个尽责的同事！

I will await your phone call.

Kind regards

3. 如果我是 D，看到以下这封 K 的邮件我可能会哭着高呼："领导英明，我必以死相随。"

Dear ××,

That has make me so surprised and disappointment when I saw YYY's email. Pls take exactly immediate action to push all thing come back the right way.

建议大家多用"surprised and disappointed"这两个高雅地表达不满的词。

I am really appreciated for D has strictly complied with company's policy. And pls clearly to be noted, all her previous and coming actions are under my authorization!

看到没，这才是好老板！这里的潜台词是：老外你别搞分化，是我让她这样做的，怎么样？

Here I would like to list the details again, even though D has shown your side for many times.

QC inspection for TCS:

All of us know well about Q, and they represent the authority in the field. The end customer has enough confidence to them. I have been working together them in the past several years, and really know well for all the procedure. So I think that is no necessary from your side to doubt their QC report.

For make all things come back on the road, and show our strong willing to continue the business I would like to show our procedure (we only accept this solution at this moment):...

（不列出来了。）

先说明为何我方坚持不让你的人来重验，因为最终客户指定的第三方 Q 已经验过了，你还吵什么吵？然后给出一个轻微的让步，大家看着办，有个台阶下。

We believe above solution is our final accepting solution, and would not accept any future re-negotiation.

坚定且有礼貌。

I would like to reiterate here, D has my all authority under handling this issue. For any future connection pls contact with her directly.

Regards,

K

故事还在继续，但我觉得这个例子我们看到这里就够了。双方的邮件都不错，表达的方式值得大家学习。

质量投诉该如何处理

这一部分的内容是品质管理。工厂远非完善，品质投诉天天都有，我们怎样有效沟通呢？下面是一个很好的例子。

这个例子出现在一种近年比较常见的外贸模式——网店直供。我有理由怀疑，你们可能大大低估了这种生意模式的综合成本，从而被老外占了大便宜。C端奇葩多、问题杂，这个管理成本不是长期做B端的你能理解的。你帮老外直接发货，他验也不验，责任百分之百在你身上，有问题你每条都得回答，帮他做客服（他忙起来也不在乎你的英文表达能力）。这个例子就是这样一个问题。

背景如下。

客户是以色列人，在美国做电商。在销售第二批货时，他的一位买家向他反映产品上有疑似血的物质。

我发了下面两封邮件解答。

第一封：

Hi,

　　Is it other case picture?[1]

Let me introduce mirror stainless steel manufacture process.[2]

1. 把"case picture"改为"picture showing defects"比较好。
2. 是"SS mirror"还是"mirror SS"，我猜这是个镜子吧？"introduce"这样用可以，但如果是我，我会说

Ⅰ. Selecting stainless steel plate, about 1m × 1m size.

Ⅱ. Join the red grinding material in grinding machine.

Ⅲ. Grinding out mirror plate.

Ⅳ. Cleaning and cover film.[1]

This process is finished[2] in grinding factory. We usually send to grind 100-400 pcs steel plates in one time.[3]

In order to protect surface, when we get back stainless steel, it covers film. We can't test it is clean or not. If it doesn't clean carefully or deeply, it remains a bit red on surface. When workers pack it, they can't remove film to check it is clean or not.[4]

"let me explain", 也不为什么, 我看到所有人都这样用, BE是靠积累和沉淀的。

1. 非常粗糙的过程, 看场合用。C端客户可能就够了。

2. 注意, "finished"有另外一个意思, 特别是在这个例子中。"finish"可以是表面处理"finishing", 你的镜子是要做"finishing"的。你在这里究竟是指"完成"还是"表面处理"呢? 如果表示"完成"的话, 用"completed"吧。

3. 不是"on time", 而是"per lot", 即每批次。

4. 这里, 如果本叔是位普通的顾客, 可能就算了。可是我是一位熟悉运营操作的买家, 你的这个理由我完全不能接受。你在覆胶膜前就不能确保品质吗? 这是一个质

I always tell grinding factory to keep clean on steel plate. It maybe happen on several discu in a batch.[1]

Thoroughly solve this question, worker remove film when packing, but it will remain some fingerprints on mirror. In past time,[2] it happens little this case.[3]

If it happens, I will replace new unit to you. Waiting for your comments.

Thank you,

L

量系统误差。不懂的人就让你过了，但是懂品管的人是不会轻易放过你的。

1. 我看到一位苦口婆心的中介，有心无力地恪守他工作的本分。你总是说工厂要做好事情，可是你无能为力。看，又多了一个老外要直接找工厂的原因，怎么破解？

2. "in the past" 就够了，没有 "in past time" 这个说法。

3. 你是想说以往很少出现这样的情况吗？

第二封：

Hi,

The red had two possibilities, blood or red grinding material remain.

I am not sure according your picture. If it is blood, it happens when packing, workers hand is cut by edge. So the edge is red.[4] If edge is clean and middle part is red, I think it

4. 你可能低估了如果红色污迹真的是血的严重性，血是传染病的媒介，可以申索的赔偿非同小可，不是你不要货就能解决的。

is possible red grinding remain. The second case is difficult to find when it covers film. I demand workers to clean discs with towel before packing.

Waiting for your suggestion.

Thank you,

L

要重写这封邮件，难度在于解读的人是否专业，是B端客户还是C端客户。但从内容来看，这是给B端客户的，那我们就针对这个受众改写吧。

回复电邮时，建议大家先用中文理清思路，用自己的文字先把逻辑写出来。

1. 问题发生了，不知是真是假，别急着道歉，态度要积极，不卑不亢。要多了解情况，与B端客户是合作关系，他有责任提供足够的咨询供你研究。

2. 针对问题点解释一下工艺，网友做对了。

3. 提出可能性。

4. 跟进计划。

参考范文如下。

Hi,

Well received and thanks for the defect information. The red stain seems scary[1] and it

1. 业务员，特别是女孩子，可以在专业的基础上加上一点人性，例如"哎呀，那么可怕"。

is really something uncommon to us. I would like to have some more detailed pictures to discuss with our quality manager.[1] Be assured that we take this as a priority and you can expect a solution from us soon.

From what I see in the picture, my gut feeling[2] is that it is not blood—as you suggested. It does look like some grinding remains from the process, which match the color pretty well. Let me explain to you the process.[3]

Although the manufacturing process is under strict control, it is not perfect.[4] Chances are that workers failed to clean it by mistake and the inspector failed to track it down.

My immediate action is to:

Ⅰ. Make clear the source of the problem.

Ⅱ. Define responsibility[5] and make necessary compensation.

Ⅲ. Improve our process to make sure this is the last time we will be having this problem. Yet I need your help to provide more details of

1. 你要记住，不要自己去处理品质问题。为什么？因为你还不够资格！你后面应该有一支专业的队伍在支持你，而你在老外面前，应该是那位在中国为客户争取利益的好同志。
2. "gut feeling"是什么？它的意思是"我瞎猜的"。你能瞎猜吗？能！你作为个人可以，但你的公司不能瞎猜。听明白我这句话的就去用这个招吧。
3. 这里就不详细写过程了。
4. 这一点是可以承认的。世事没有完美，虽说过程让事情有根据，但也会有出错的时候，这些事，老手们都懂。
5. "Define"这个词经常用，不只是用在这里。再说，"define"谁不懂？BE只需要用简单的词汇。

the course and let's fix the problem together.¹

Regards,

Ben

> 相信我写了那么多，真没几个生字是你不懂的，但这些简单的字用在一起就是魔法了，是不是？
> 1. 这才是正确的人生态度！

本部分建议掌握的 BE 金句

1. Be assured that we take this as a priority and you can expect a solution from us soon.
2. Although the manufacturing process is under strict control, it is not perfect.

八级英语为什么写不出好 BE

下面要讲的例子是一个八级英语的网友的作品。"英文好不代表商业英文好"，这个观点可以说在这个案例中体现得淋漓尽致。整篇文稿用字优美，文法我只抓到一个小错，估计这个网友在学校拿过奖学金。我看网友已经努力不单纯地搬字过纸了，可是还只是停留在翻译阶段，老板说什么就译什么。她的工作虽然完成了，但在表达上可以更好。

我们来看看例子。下面是网友老板的原话。

经过我司汇总2015年9月至12月的客诉发现，98%的不良产品都是由我司外观检测疏忽所致，我首先以我个人的名义向你致以最诚挚的歉意，并对贵司采用全检方式收下这批货物表示感谢。我司将会承担挑选费和不良数量赔偿。

为了保证质量，避免不良产品外流至客户端，我司已经出台外观检测标准，加强QC培训并采取员工绩效考核制度。在此，也非常希望贵司能再给我司机会，我们保证以后提供的产品绝不会再有类似的情况发生。谢谢理解！

下面是网友的英文稿。

After carefully summarizing the claims[1] from your side[2] dated from September 2015 to December 2015, we are sorry to find that 98% of the defective products are due to our negligence[3] during the appearance inspection.[4] Here I would like to extend my sincerest apologies to you, on behalf of ××company and myself. At the same time, we want to thank you for your effort to inspect all the products.

1. "经我司小心汇总"，字面译得完全没错，只能说感觉怪怪的。
2. "your side"的意思是"你那边"，很中式。
3. "negligence"是法律用语，写合同时用的，这里的语气不需要那么重。
4. 一般"目视检测"会用"visual inspection"，这是品管学用语，八级英语不会教。

We are going to take¹ all the charges for selecting² and compensate you for your loss caused by the defective products.

To ensure quality³ ×× has already introduced strict appearance inspection standards (since ××), which has be⁴ constantly used to train and evaluate every employee.⁵

We are now confident that defective product will be rejected⁶ before shipping to our customers. Here, I very much hope that you could give us another chance to cooperate with each other. We guarantee that similar situation will never occurs again in the future.⁷

Thank you for kind understanding!

1. 我会把这句改为"We will be responsible for"，这样更直接，听起来胸怀更大，更有责任感。
2. 用"screening"专业一点。
3. 这里又要用到一个八级英语没教的专业品管措辞，改为"As part of our quality assurance system"，你的格局就大多了！
4. 应为"has been"，我文法那么差都能找到错，但是只要不影响理解就行，我只是在鸡蛋里挑骨头。
5. 不是"employee"，而是"workers"，你不会去教门卫和保洁这个标准。
6. 你们下了那么多功夫，不就是为了挑选坏品吗？品质是生产出来的！
7. 如何保证呢？我只看到你们说会培训员工、加强检查……说真的，任何一个懂行的品质经理都不会轻易放过你们。

"品质是生产出来的"是多么重要又多么容易被忽视的概念啊！不过，真不怪这个网友，他刚出学校不久，根本不可能懂。也不怪老板，没有几个老板真的什么都懂。那怪谁？品管经理！我看这真是概念的问题。这些年来我看到很多品管经理，出了事就只懂"返工""加强检查"，动不动就"提高工人意识"，没事就挂些口号，如"品质是我们的生命"。品质的重点是在一个合理设计的生产流程下，反复在流程中检测错误，就算最笨的工人也没有办法把事情搞砸，这才叫作"品质生产"！品质，靠的不是工匠精神，也不是老板和工人的良心，靠的只有一个：流程！

参考范文如下。

On behalf of the ×× company and with deepest regrets,[1] I would like to express my sincerest apology regarding the quality defect dated Sep. to Dec., 2015. We will be responsible for all the necessary costs including screening and logistic cost due to the delay.[2]

1. 意思是深感遗憾，一个外交辞令用在这封比较正式的邮件中，很合适。
2. 注意：如果这样写，你必须清楚你将要承担的责任可能会非常大。因为"delay"和"defect"可以引申到很多索偿。如果没有这个打算，就别写得那么厉害。

Within ××, I've demanded[1] to setup a cross functional team leaded by our quality VP and championed[2] by myself, with an aim to investigate the situation and focus on the improvement plan. We are looking into the very fine details[3] of the whole manufacturing process and will implement procedure including visual inspection,[4] acceptance standard review, workers training and so on. Yet, our aim is to work out the best manufacturing process instead of keeping screening and rejecting. A full improvement report is expected by the end of this week.

This is our fault and I humbly[5] ask for your forgiveness and the opportunity to show our improvement. We learn from mistakes and we are confident that this will not happen again.

1. 又一个既浅白又强大的字：demand。我以前收到过老板在正式邮件上写"I demand Ben to..."霸气！
2. "champion"指你们什么都懂，但在这里又是一个高级用法。大概有监督的意思，但不是自己动手，很高，很500强。
3. "very"的另一种用法，"the very next day"，学英文的网友可能会懂。
4. 不用"appearance"，改用"visual"，正如你不会对一个熟悉红茶的朋友说我要一杯茶，而是我要大吉岭……
5. 不一定是威灵顿大公跪在不列颠国王前说的那句"as your humble servant"，"humble"是一个非常适合用来表达"坦诚"的词。请别问我为什么这不解释为谦虚。

本叔好像很少用这种坦诚的文字。不过真的做错事时就要收起霸气，好好认错，以改进为目的，而不是第一时间推卸责任。

REALLY GOOD NEWS
YOU WANT TO EXPAND YOUR MARKET

第4章 报　　价

在回文中，可以按照一个比例做回应。八成是回答老外的问题，两成是策略性文字。这是什么意思？很有针对性地说说你究竟有多适合成为他的供应商。

报价单要怎样写？这个太简单了，目前已经有很多人在教，本叔就不教了。但如何利用发报价单的那封电邮多争取几份订单，我在本章第四部分写得挺详细的。

本章第一部分也是跟报价有关的——如果客户发的RFQ很详细，你可以怎样应对？

围绕报价的BE不会太多，因为大部分例子我都归类到了"价格"一项。本章第三部分是报价后关于付款账期的谈判，DDU是怎么谈的，实战性很强。

这是真客户吗

你心目中的采购经理是什么模样的？是一副大爷的嘴脸，还是口若悬河的雄辩家？有人会说：我的客户很好啊！又有人会说：我的客户跟我私底下相处还行，但人多时他就是另一个人了。其实很简单，一个好的采购经理是多面的，有需要时可以哭，可以怒，可以感恩，可以友善。我们都是当演员的料。

说说这次的例子。当我还在500强当采购时，大规模的项目都会正式地用报价请求文件（request for quotation，RFQ），就算是小项目，我也习惯于把大量背景写出来，因为：

1. 我一次性写出来，不至于每个工厂都来问我一遍，我懒得回答。
2. 我们采购有责任把正确的信息尽量清楚、详细地告诉供应商，这叫专业。

3. 我经常看到一些业务员在评论我的文章时说"问那么多，客户会觉得你烦"之类的话，这只能说明他还没见过世面。至于问题有多详细，有点像以下例子中这个客户那样。

Hi 本叔，

以下是开发信回来的客户邮件，可是我发邮件过去之后就没再收到他的任何信息，不知道是哪里出问题了。但是我们的产品太多，也不可能按他要求的给他做完整的价表。

客户邮件如下。

Hello C,

Thank you very much for attention to this email.

My name is B and I'm the Operations Manager for ××.

比起那些一封电邮只说"send me your best price"那种客户，这个礼貌多了。不过，这封电邮有点怪，看下去。

We are a large wholesale supplier to the promotional products industry, supplying distributors in the industry and not end users.

原来是做促销品的。这个行业的特点是不停地需要新的供应商。对新供应商友善是工作的一部分……

We have been in business over 16 years, and we are highly respected with our current suppliers and have A+ credit ratings with both our domestic and overseas vendors.

这个 A+ 不用太认真，除非它是国际认可的标准，例如 D&B。

We have our own company and 2 other associated family businesses both doing very high volumes in the promotional product industry.

We advertise through trade organizations very heavily and produce up to 70-75 orders per day, with about 1/3 of these orders being ×× items.

看到这里，我感觉老外有点太详细了。

At the moment we are currently in the middle of a major advertising campaign to build our ×× business further, so we are very serious about our investment in this area.

We are very please with our current factory, however we're researching other factories currently because our business is expending rapidly, and we would like to establish a business relationship with another vendor.

这里老外给人的感觉太老实，我特别不习惯，仿佛看到一个老好人在后面对你微笑一样，或者是奸笑。

We're interested in receiving more information about your factory's customer service, product quality, lead times, pricing, and shipping costs. Please also advise if your factory provides any rush services on lapel pins or any other products.

这里明确地列出了他的要求。

The majority of our products orders ship directly to our warehouse (zip code ××) via Fedex/UPS priority international as a bulk shipment and then we handle the shipping to our clients from our warehouse.

We will provide your factory with camera ready artwork for the proofs. Please kindly advise the turnaround time to receive a proof.

太详细了，不过我也真的见过一些说得过度详细的老外。

If your pricing is good, and we continue our discussion about doing business together, we will have to have a valid Price Sheet from your factory. We simply do to much business to receive pricing from you on a case by case basis.

这句话老外也错文法了，这挺正常的，不要介意。BE 主要看的不是这些。

Please provide us with a shipping quotation if possible, or please advise if your pricing already includes the shipping costs.

It would be great to get set up with you and try out your services.

We have a large product range which includes ××. So if there is any other products you can provide us with information on please do so.

这是促销品行业的一贯做法，他们需要很多不同的新产品。

Get back to me as soon as possible and let's start a dialogue. Thank you.

这封邮件有点详细得可怕，有点像编出来的，但我又不觉得他说的是假的，可能是因为我明白他为什么要这样做。然而如果我是业务员的话，我还是会留一个心眼。

以下是网友的回复。

Hello B,

Thanks for kindly introduction on you and your esteemed company.

"esteemed company" 不算是低声下气地说话，但用语重了点，可以用，但不太建议。

It's great to know your main business and we do hope to establish long term win-win business relationship with your esteemed company and become your stable and reliable supplier in China.

"stable and reliable" 赞一个，而不是 "cheap and best friend in China"。

For ×× products, we have more advantages of bulk production, quick turnaround and excellent quality guarantee.

1. For ××1 items, × days for samples and × days for mass production (it will be rechecked based on detailed design & quantity).

For × products, × days for samples and × days for mass production (depends on design & quantity as well).

Rush lead time on all items are firmly supported without extra charge.

2. For the every beginning stage, we appreciate your detailed design inquiries or trial order for evaluation. For the following cooperation, price list will be arranged corresponding for your regular orders.

3. Regarding shipment by UPS (priority service), the rough freight

is as below.

    A. within 20kg   US$25/0.5kg + US$4.30/0.5kg (eg. 3kg：US$25+ US$4.3 ×2.5×2 = US$46.50)

    B. 21-44kg   US$6.0/kg

    C. 45-70kg   US$5.7/kg

    D. over 71kg   US$5.40/kg

我都看晕了，强烈建议你列表说明，而不是用文字。

4. We are always responsible for our customers.

（1）X - Keep for 3 years since the last date of shipment

（2）Free Artwork services

（3）Quality- strictly follow order instruction and approved artwork.

（4）No MOQ for all items

（5）Welcome to visit us once you and your team come to China.

这里也不错，我看出了服务。

Looking forward to our next dialogue.

整体上，这还算是个不错的回复。可是，这叫作一问一答。人家问多少，你就答多少。在回文中，可以按照一个比例做回应，八成是回答老外的问题（尽量一条一条全部回答。我见过太多问三条只回答一条的供应商），两成是策略性文字。这是什么意思？你就不想做一个有互动的供应商吗？你就不想很有针对性地说说你究竟有多适合成为他的供应商吗？我指的是"针对性"，而不是那种要跟人家"establish long term relationship"的陈词滥调。

那么如何有针对性？打开客户的网页慢慢看，既然是有两三家公司的组织，那么其网站上会有足够的资料让你研究，好好了解吧。

此处就不再列举范文了，以英文的角度，这一篇还算可以。

如何解释报价

关于这个问题，我可以吐槽好久。

我都不记得我收过多少奇形怪状的报价单了。业务员没事就来跟我扯家常，但报价时拖拖拉拉甚至不接我电话的情况都有。当我三催四请后，他们发过来的报价单让我看到"吐血"。为了证明不只是我一个人有这样的看法，我把某不知名采购顾问公司前线采购员的话放在下面。

某采购顾问公司：（看完报价单后）这PI上的银行信息特别复杂，让人很迷惑，到底是私人账号还是公户付款？

某采购顾问公司：（发来报价单）这个是好久之前的了。

某采购顾问公司：有规格、价格和有效期，这些都不错，但是最好有生产交货期、样品价格和样品交货期。目前汇率不稳定，最好也加上按当前的汇率以及报价人的联系方式。

设想一下，采购员等了你的报价好几天，等来的却是个不完整的报价，你叫我怎样用来比较，怎样跟内部同事交代？然后我又要苦心把每个问题问一次：你这个价格是多少量的呀？FOB（free on board）

还是EXW（ex works）？这一等，又是好几天……这样的情况非常普遍，以至于有些特别急、特别重要的项目，我都用RFQ。我把格式做好，然后让供应商填写。很多时候即使这样还不够，因为供应商又会说这不明白那不明白……明明都写得很清楚了，还是会问。

你可能会问："采购哪有那么好呀，我的客户都懒得要死。"怎么说呢，这件事就好像夫妻俩，老公把厕所打扫了，老婆会觉得厕所很干净不用打扫了；要是夫妻俩都懒，那么厕所一定很可怕；而双方的沟通更可怕，你可能根本不能觉察到。采购不花时间和精力去理清信息，那么将来就会有不必要的误会，损失可能很严重。你的客户懒，可能只是因为他不专业，也可能是他不需要专业……

目前已经有不少书、文章、课程……都在教你如何报价，我觉得没必要教大家怎样写一张报价单。相反，大部分人都不懂得把握机会，在发报价单的那封电邮上做一做文章，只会写"attached please find our quotation for your kind, very kind, kind kind kind reference"，然后是"let me know if you have any question"。你就不能把你的报价单做得没什么"question"，连"let you know"都没机会，一步到位吗？服务！这才是服务啊！

我把大家很多时候都不记得放入报价单的要点列出来，大家以后可以根据情况使用。

1. 有效期（validity）。报价都该有个期限，不是常常有人说："老外对我们加价很不满。可是那是去年的价格啊！现在材料那么贵，怎么办？"如果你的工厂或车间上个月刚报完价，你现在去问他，他却摊手说"加价了,怪我吗",你会怎样?这些事情,只要白纸黑字在报价单上写个有效期,你就大有理由说加价是正常的。再者,你加个有效期,是不是能在老外迟迟不下单时,提醒他一下?这总比你苦苦想个开场白又怕人家觉得你烦要好得多。

2. 汇率(exchange rate)。我的主要采购经验来自量大款少(high volume low mix,HVLM)的行业。原材料价格和汇率这两项都是我特别关心的事情。在这个行业,报价都会写上这两项基准,例如,铜价 $××/吨,美元对人民币 6.×……这样很好,大家不用每次为这两项调价而重新谈判,只需要根据一个双方同意的公式,浮动超过一定范围之后就差不多是自动调价了。我们把这叫作"price adjustment mechanism",是一个"mechanism",一个机制,是说自动就调价了。这对大家也是个好的参考。如果不写,那么你每次都去跟老外谈加价,每次都会谈得不开心吧。

3. 交货标准周期(delivery lead time)。交货期是针对个别送货安排的,如 20 Sep. 到达宁波港。但如果是生产周期,那么就每次都能用上。交货标准周期跟生产周期又不同,以后有机会再教。报价单上应该写上相关产品的交货标准周期,例如,定金后 20 天发货,定制加 5 天,诸如此类。

4. 保质期(shelf life)。某些产品会有保质期,最简单的就是食品类,但你不要在报价单上写一个确切的时间(例如,25/11/2018),而是写上一个时间间隔(time interval),如 18 个月。因为虽然你现在报价,但要等人家下单了你才知道会何时生产,否则除非你做假。将保质期写在报价单上只是个提醒，我不认为是必需的，因为这是产品资料的范围了，不属于商业条件之一。不过我见过不少次有人写上，对于买家来说还是挺方便的，所以建议写上。

5. 保养期（warranty）。这是个售后的概念，同上，这属于产品资料，但写在报价单上，人家看来就专业多了。正如大部分营销方法一样，说与不说，本身就是个区别。

6. 银行账户（Bank A/C）。这个问题，我年少无知时遇到过下单后付钱时才出现问题，开户名称跟公司名不一样。这对买家是个大风险！万一供应商说没收过钱呢？业务员一般都会来请我抽烟，然后扯今年公司交了很多税了，要想想办法什么的。这件事，难道你就认为我不知道你可能正在飞单？为了杜绝这些破事，后来我一律不接受私人账户，只做公账交易。

其他我没提到的，我叫作基本条件。最少订单量（minimum order quantity，MOQ）、大货价格、样板价、日期什么的，我就不提了。到范文时间了，这次是一位港资公司的业务经理写给一位他刚刚见过面的采购总监的报价电邮。本来这只是发一个报价单而已，但这位经理把握每次沟通的机会去展现自己的优势和服务，所以连一封电邮都写得很清晰。

Hi Ben,

Nice meeting you in the airport. It was short but helpful for us to understand the opportunity to work with Zecker.

> 这种电邮的开端很适合提起一些往事，一些能让人回想起的往事，如我们一起看过的海……

According to our conversation, I would like to present you our offer[1] of producing the handle-set by our Dongguan facility as attached. We understand this is one of your key product line and is suitable as a reference to demonstrate our competitiveness.[2]

To make the quotation clearer, hereby I highlight some key messages for your quick reference:[3]

Ⅰ. The quotation is valid for 3 months, starting from the date of the quotation.

Ⅱ. The price is based on the exchange rate of 1:6.×, from USD to RMB.

Ⅲ. The price is based on brass at $×× per ton.

1. 我不会用"send you our quotation"这么粗糙的文字。"present"和"offer"都不是什么生词，你应该本来就懂，只是你不会用而已。读完我的BE，你一定能发现你根本没有必要死记生词。

2. 这是一个好的切入策略，用一个主力产品型号报价能让人易于比较，也容易产生印象。当然，如果你本来就没什么价格优势，再好的文字都帮不了你。

3. 这里要小心一点。"highlight"的意思是把报价单档案内已经有的内容的重点再说一次。千万不要在这里写一些报价单上没有的新内容。不然会产生误会，千万注意！

Ⅳ. Our standard delivery lead-time is 35 days upon written confirmation. This could be clearly improved with a liable forecast provided by you.[1]

Ⅴ. We offer 2 years warranty service on finished goods unless otherwise stated.[2]

Ⅵ. Pls find our Chinese Hong Kong bank account as written on the quotation. It is under the name of our Chinese Hong Kong entity which solely own our facilities in Chinese mainland, including the said one in Dongguan.[3]

1. 对我来说，预测必须是有责任的。不然老外乱估一通我还能给他备货吗？没有责任的预测也不是完全没用，但不建议用来做你们备货的计划。因为我见过这些预测是如何荒谬地被制定出来。只有负责，负财务责任的预测，你才可以用来做备货、备料之用。你的老板会感谢我这一番话。
2. 一般来说，"warranty"只用于成品。
3. 这里重学三个单词。第一个是"entity"，为什么不说"company"？因为"entity"是一个法律用语，用在这个情况中是完全匹配的。第二个是"solely"，完全地、全资地拥有。第三个是"facility"，我不说"factory"，不说"manufacturer"，因为都没有"facility"合适。工厂是

The cost-based quotation[1] could reflect our supply chain competent. We could of course provide you more quotation of your products if you are interested. I would also like to personally invite you[2] to visit our facility so as to understand us better.

Looking forward to hear from you.

Regards,

Franck

"facility",仓库也是"facility"。同时,在会计角度,"facility"等于"asset"(资产)。你要是改为"our Hong Kong company which completely own our factory"也行。简单是最好的,是不是一眼就看出不同?

1. 我强调这是个"cost-based"报价单,是因为我想强调,这是一个用来给老外你了解我们工厂的成本水平的报价单,我这是老实价,没有什么水分。我记得有一篇 BE 投稿花了很大篇幅说自己的价位已经是成本价了,倒不如用一句"cost-based quotation"带过。

2. 邀请客户看厂时可以友好一点、热情一点,当然也看客户是谁……

希望这一部分能帮助你改掉发不清不楚的报价单的坏习惯。有时不是你不小心，而是你根本没这个概念。现在有了，是不是专业很多？这是 BE 的功效。

> **本部分建议掌握的 BE 金句**
>
> 1. We understand this is one of your key product line and is suitable as a reference to demonstrate our competitiveness.
> 2. Our standard delivery lead-time is ×× days upon written confirmation. This could be clearly improved with a liable forecast provided by you.
> 3. The cost-based quotation could reflect our supply chain competent.

DDU 怎么谈才好

这一部分是来自门徒俱乐部的例子，属于商务条件谈判。我们来看看怎样才是"晓之以理，动之以情"。BE 用得好，就必须两者兼备。

本叔你好！

我看了你的 BE，很精彩。我的背景很简单。客户要 DDU 模式到付，我们一般是 100% 发货前付清，鸿沟啊！

我之前跟客户拉锯过一次了，各种招数我都用过了，还说公司之前有过一个没有收回货款的例子，所以现在只接受前TT，能扯的理由基本都扯过了。客户稍微动摇了一点，但最后还是回归了原位。

我默默跟进，有点死嗑的味道，因为我心里总感觉这个客户的付款方式也不是完全改变不了的。我反思之前的邮件都不是很理想。后来我又收到该客户的询盘，他还是问付款方式能不能接受。

以下是我的回复，自我感觉比之前进步了很多，但是我还是觉得挺生硬的。

客户邮件如下。

Hi,
I am about ready to place more orders for 4mm white?
Let me know if you are interested in doing business with us.
Material to be paid upon arrival.

我的回复如下。

Hi,
Very glad to get your 2nd inquiry.

To be honest, our standard payment terms is 100% prepaid before loading.（30% deposit before production + 70% balance paid before loading.）I don't want you think we are too rigid, but actually this is also the standard terms in our industry.

这段不错，不是英文不错，而是看到了诚意。"standard term"不要乱吹，真的是行业标准才这样说，不然客户看到其他供应商不是这个标准时会发怒。

I've do my best to persuade our management to meet your request, but it's too hard for us to fully accept your way. I hope you can understand my thoughts.

你不解释为什么不能接受，只说向高层争取过了，说服力不够。不过好像比说"我跟老板说了下，他就答应减价了"要好很多。

We cherish every customer, so below is our solutions for you:

"cherish"用词不错。

25% deposit before production, we also need deposit to pay our raw material supplier, 75% balance paid 15 days after see the copy of bill of lading.

注意，你这句话像是在说，我的物料成本只占25%，剩余的除了人工就是利润。哇，1元的料4元卖出去，暴利啊……另外，客户可能会觉得：你这是什么破公司，都没钱买料了，我还敢用你吗？

At this way you will pay balance when material almost arrive at you. I hope this make you feel much better.

I understand as a serious buyer you may worry about our quality, my suggestion is you can request a third party to inspect goods before shipment, we will do shipment until get approval from your inspection. We welcome inspections before shipments, this help assured for both buyers and us. Or you can place a trial order to check our quality and services before place regular orders.

感觉除了品质外，他在乎的还有其他东西。你先别一厢情愿地以为人家对你的品质没信心……还是你自己没信心？

I hope this time can make you satisfied.

单从英文来说，本篇不过不失。不过，我再三强调，BE 的 B 比 E 重要，意思是说，回复时的思维比用语重要。不知读者是否发现，回文完全没提及客户要求中的一个要点：DDU。

我估计少于 20% 的业务员做过 DDU 的单，而要求过供应商做 DDU 的人也一定不多。做之前，你先要明白一点：为什么客户要做 DDU？

我把维基百科里 DDU 的定义抄了下来，如下。

DDU—Delivered Duty Unpaid（named place of destination）.

This term means that the seller delivers the goods to the buyer to the named place of destination in the contract of sale. A transaction in international trade where the seller is responsible for making a safe delivery of goods to a named destination, paying all transportation and customs clearance expenses but not the duty. The seller bears the risks and costs associated with supplying the goods to the delivery location, where the buyer becomes responsible for paying the duty and taxes.

简单地说，DDU 是指除了客户当地关税之外的所有费用，都由供应商负责。我第一次接触 DDU 是在某 500 强位于厦门保税区的组装工厂。参照 VMI（vendor managed inventory）/JIT（just in time）的模式，我们要求供应商报价必须以 DDU 来报。结果是，大的供应商还好，小的供应商我都得花不少时间去解释这跟 FOB（free on board）有什么分别。在中国外贸界，绝大部分人都还是只会做 FOB，连 CIF（cost, insurance and freight）都不想包。（别误会，这不一定是坏事！）所以 DDU 这个"全包"的定义把很多供应商都吓退了。

为什么买家/客户方要求 DDU 呢？一个原因是风险，特别是未试过在本国以外的地方进口一些不是太懂的产品，买方怕有任何不可预计的风险时，DDU 是最安全的。假如中间突然来个海关抽验费用，成本都能转嫁给供应商。

另一个原因我说了你都不信：懒！老外懒得去查中间还有什么别的费用，反正你就报送到我家门口的费用就行了。

所以我们回这封信时也应该把 DDU 的要点概括进去。我凭直觉判断，这个客户这次要求 100% DDU 货到付款的原因，并非在于现金流问题，而是风险！这位网友一直坚持死磕的力度，可能用在错的方向上了！他一直只说自己的公司如何受过伤，却没帮老外想如何降低风险。

我认为逻辑应该是这样的：

1. 你的单我当然是接定了，现在只剩下一个简单的技术性问题，我们可以谈谈。

2. 我们没做过 DDU，不过我查了，以下是所有费用的清单。

3. 您看看其实也不是那么危险。

4. 风险是对等的，我们也有担心的问题。

5. 所以，一人让一步吧。

晓之以理，以上逻辑就是理。接下来就看你的 BE 如何动之以情了。以下是参考范文。

Hi,

Of course I am ready to take your order. We've spent long time together trying to make things happen and I am sure we can figure it out.[1]

As an industrial norm,[2] 100% payment before shipment has it reasoned. If you are so kind[3] to put yourself into my shoes: you get a paper or just a verbal confirmation from customers and then you start to spend money on material and processing. Until the goods arrive at your customer you don't get anything back. The risk and the cash cycle are just too much for us.[4]

We also notice your request for DDU term. To be frank we don't normally work under this term simply because we don't understand the risk behind it.[5] In order to win your order[6] we have seriously looked into it and will work together with a logistic provider who has good experience and presence in your

1. 聊聊战斗友谊，不过这一段不是所有情况都适合。有时你想拉近距离，有时你却是想怎样保持礼貌的距离，这一点要你自己决定。
2. "norm"跟"standard"差不多，不过"standard"是个比较科学和生硬的字。
3. 这里我用了你们一直很爱用的"kind"。
4. 要让他明白你的处境，这个"put yourself into my shoes"挺好用的。
5. 不明白这个风险，所以我们很少做DDU，非常合理。
6. 我是有多想要你的订单啊！

country.¹ I have done a total cost breakdown for your reference as attached hoping to make our cost structure more visualized to you.²

We've been looking for a reasonable middle way that balances our risk and cost, and here is the proposal:³

Ⅰ. We need ××% of deposit to kick off this project and to cover all the related cost (material + overhead).

Ⅱ. We will do DDU, as you wish.⁴ We will cover part of your risk.

Ⅲ. Feel free to arrange 3rd party inspection if it is necessary. However I personally don't think it is a must. We have a quality system that you can trust.⁵

Ⅳ. We offer extra 15 days for your incoming inspection before paying us the balance. This will make sure you have enough time to check and reduce your quality risk.⁶

1. 你要说明，你找的不是一个一般的三流物流公司。它是专业的，更重要的是熟悉贵国情况。
2. 这才是服务！不是你嘴上常说的服务好，而是实际解决客户痛点，为客户提供增值服务。
3. 列举要点是最有条理的表达方法。
4. "as you wish"，如你所愿。
5. 你可以派人来，但我觉得没这个必要。
6. 我已经仁至义尽了。

This is by far the best deal we've offered.
I hope this time we could start the business.
    Regards,
    Ben

REALLY GOOD NEWS
YOU WANT TO EXPAND YOUR MARKET

第 5 章 交 货 期

我初入行做采购时,不是特别明白自己的责任,为了安全,往往习惯于把标准定得很高、很死,这样不准、那样不行。到了后来才明白,我的责任是去解决问题,而不是当一只看门狗。

两个重量级"绵里藏针"的例子都是跟交货期有关的,想一想也不无道理。货交不出,急起来绝大部分人都会先保护自己(而不是去解决问题),不论责任是谁的,对方都会指责你。这时 BE 就起了很大的作用——反击!一篇好的 BE 可以让你不用赔款,把白纸黑字的证据升华演绎,成为保护你自己和公司利益的利器!在本章的第一部分,老外根本不问是非就把责任推到供货方身上,供货方要是乖乖认错就笨了,因为这是不可抗力,要怎么打好这手牌?去读一读吧。

买方指鹿为马这件事并不新鲜,特别是当他急起来的时候,为了不丢掉工作,什么事都做得出来。白纸黑字是最重要的,如何破解?请看看本章第二部分。

厦门刮台风,不可抵抗与只懂说不的客户

我初入行做采购时,不是特别明白自己的责任,为了安全,往往习惯于把标准定得很高、很死,这样不准、那样不行。十多年前当采购确实是"优差",我说一句"不能接受",人家就得花很大力气改过(要放在现在,恐怕供应商都不会理你)。到了后面我才明白,我的责任是去解决问题,而不是当一只看门狗。要达到职业成熟,还是需要一个过程的。

这次的例子是:台风过后,劫后余生,货品受损,交期无法如期。客户死活不接受,不管网友怎样说都没用。网友不知所措,来稿给我

看有没有招。那么我就试试给点思路，看看是否能参考一下。

我一直很佩服你的 BE 高度，你的 BE 我一直在读，还做了收藏。我碰到了突发情况，实在想不到比较好的解决方法，也不知道怎么回复客户。可否耽误你几分钟时间帮我看一下这个问题？以下是问题和背景介绍。

产品：服装，需要用到面料和罩杯，流程是先订购面辅料，再生产成衣；G20 会议后，因为环保原因暂停了不少生产面料的工厂，现在面料供应特别紧张。

客户：美国进口商。

付款方式：零预付，客户收到货后付款。

问题：9 月 15 日福建遭受特大台风，工厂和仓库严重受损，面料和罩杯都被水泡了，导致我们按原计划进行成衣生产，原定的交货期无法履行，交货期推后是肯定的，新的交货期起码需要 4 天左右才能核算出来。(当地的水电今早已停止供应，需要等水电恢复，结合工厂情况才能给出新的安排计划。)

今早我给客户发邮件，说明我们碰到的突发情况，并提供了受灾照片和新闻报道，希望能延迟交货。客户回复不接受交货期延误，并说我们的进度一直滞后，且缺乏责任感。

作为供货方，我们理解因刮台风受灾不关客户的事情，客户也没有义务理解和同情我们，而且延迟交货会影响客户自己以及他们的客户的销售计划。但是他们说的不同意延迟交货，我们目前确实无法做到。

网友的邮件如下。

Dear C,

Regarding shipment schedule updated on 9/12/16: there's some changes because of 9/15/16 typhoon in Fujian, where our fabric manufacturer located.

Some of the fabric and grey fabricate are soaked during the typhoon.

Latest shipment status might be available till earlier of next week. I will update asap.

Attached are the picture to show you the situation of the place and our ordered fabric.

I will send you relevant public news in a separate email.

Best regards,

× ×

客户很快回复,如下。

This is not fair this may make me reduce the qty ordered cause you are so late on everything I cannot accept all these sudden changes I'm in deep trouble of losing clients because of your lack of responsibility

Sent from my iPhone

下面是网友的第二封邮件——提供对应的受灾新闻,证明事情的真实性。

Dear L,

Below is the public news regarding the typhoon:

...
Most powerful typhoon since 1949 batters Fujian.
Best regards,
××

客户的回复如下。

My customers will not understand and will not care about this problem because it's not their problem business is tough and cannot delay.
Sent from my iPhone

最后是网友的回复，逻辑是这样的：表示理解客户的处境，出了这样的天灾，我们确实无能为力，但是我们会尽我们所能赶货，尽量少延误，并且尽快给客户更新最新的交货期。

Dear ,
I apologize for this delay. This is the first time I meet during my 20+ years in the industry.
We will do our best to push the production and try to arrange the shipment ASAP. New shipment schedule will be updated very soon. It should be available on next Wednesday.
Best regards

我看到这里，觉得最好是用列举要点的形式把这个例子的要点概括出来。

1. 重中之重，老外你不接受又能怎样，能起死回生吗？我从他用手机立即回复这件事，就知道他根本没用脑去试图解决问题，而是百分之百地把问题扔回给供应商。看似很对，这是供应商做错了，关自己什么事？但老外你知道什么叫"force majeure"吗？中文叫"不可抗力"。如果有合同，那么对不起，老外你因这种天灾而受到的损失并不在合同的保护范围之内。如果不顾什么长期合作、什么客户关系的话，网友根本不用理老外。帮他尽快交货，是人情；不帮他，我也没什么过错。

2. 物料进水了，他的损失是晚收货，我的损失是全批物料不能用了。所以，不要觉得我们什么都没做，他零预付款我也在帮他收拾摊子，这不是不负责任。

3. 懂得说明这一点，让他明白我现在是在帮他，他还在生什么孩子气？

4. 要赞一下，这种天灾必须要提供第三方报道。网友这次做对了。

"不可抗力"几乎所有合同上都会写，不只是天灾，某些人祸，好像动乱、政变等，也属于这个范畴。作为一个优质、负责的中国供应商，你当然也会尽力协助解决问题，但协助和责任之间的距离，你必须跟客户沟通。以下是参考范文。

Hi,

This is one of the worst typhoon I've ever seen in my life. We are definitely not the only one affected. The whole Fujian province is in a mess. Let's say, we are lucky already that the problem is visualized and we can have our hands on it.[1]

The material is soaked with water and unable to use. This is the lost we are suffering and being absorbed by our own.[2] We spoke with our insurance agency and there is nothing they could do — it is called "Forced Majeure". All contracts, including the one between us, are excluded from the responsibility caused by this typhoon.[3]

Yet, as a responsible supplier, we are still doing our best to meet your deadline, even when we have not received a penny from you.[4]

I have explained the course of action in the previous email, and I suggest you take a look on it.[5] Be assured that we work on the same objective — to satisfy your customer. I will report status again soon.

Regards,

Ben

1. 他要明白,整个福建省都有事,我们不是特例。一般来说,在灾害中能清楚地知道情况的进展也是一种本事。不信的话,老外你找其他人试试。
2. 先把自己的损失说出来。
3. 重点来了,看我如何间接又含蓄地说不关我的事,而是把保险公司拉下水,他们是最看重条款的人,然后带出"所有合同在不可抗力之下无效",这样就不像直接说"我没有责任"那么令人讨厌。
4. 最后这句太霸气了,潜台词是:"我一毛钱都没收就先损失了,你还吵什么吵。"不过,慎用!
5. 老外你自己看看,我不重打字了。

> **本部分建议掌握的 BE 金句**
>
> 1. We are lucky already that the problem is visualized and we can have our hands on it.
> 2. Be assured that we work on the same objective — to satisfy your customer.

如何对待指鹿为马的客户

前面的内容都没有涉及我心目中的"大客户行为"。这种"大客户行为"不一定是指营业额达到多少个亿的客户的行为,而是复杂的内部行为。以我自身的经验,最常见的是"中西之争"和"新旧之争"两种。一帮人极力开发新的供应商(一般在亚洲),另一帮人坚持希望继续使用旧的供应商(有时在他们本土,有时在中国)。这种事背后,不一定是你们所想的单纯为了金钱利益,而是他们自身在公司的影响力、仕途、旧人之间的感情、不愿变化的打工心态……综合而来。我的"假装在 500 强"就是在这种背景下诞生的。

这一部分所说的,貌似是单纯的交货期问题,实际上却是权力之争。作为供应商,如何能在当中如鱼得水呢?这是个政治课。BE 能教你的,没有那么多,但如何见招拆招,你是可以学会的。原文太长,以下例子有删减。

本叔好，

一个大客户，今年是第二次合作，去年第一次合作不是很顺畅，有很多因素，因此客户还是决定在欧洲当地买。今年我们主动给客户降价两次，最后终于重启合作。但是这次合作的时间又正好赶在过节。

客户在10月底确认12月的订单，交货期非常紧张。我催客户交定金两次了。

第一次我只说时间紧张，要快点。第二次我觉得要说明白点，免得将来客户怪我。于是我说如果付款不及时，生产不出来就赶不上他预定的到货时间了。

网友邮件如下。

Good morning dears,

Sorry I have to chase on the balance payment again.（Order Ref: 69946/2661077）

Let me explain to you why.

You ask 1st December container W/C 05.12.2016, we need to ship it before the end of October（No later than 29th）.

Therefore, we need to receive balance payment at 24th to ensure I can arrange the container loading on time.

Time is tight, please pay us today to help your timely delivery.

2nd December container（Offer Ref: 69957/2661942）W/C 12.12.2016. We need to ship it at the beginning of November（No later than November 5）.

Need deposit to us ASAP so I can arrange your production in advance.

Two payments at one time can save some bank charges for you.

网友：现在看好像还是说得不够明白。

客户回复如下。

L,

As advised yesterday we need to leave it till Monday and hopefully we can pay the balance of the 1st container and the deposit of the 2nd container at the same time.

网友：我看客户不着急的样子，我也没办法了，而且我开始默认客户的到货时间是可以随便改动的，于是我也不着急了。直到前两天客户终于付款了，然后就开始催交货，要求圣诞假期前到货，实情是这么短的时间我们根本生产不出来，更别说现在连订舱都快订不上了！昨晚我跟客户说明，由于节前船期紧张，到货时间必须调整为明年1月初。

本叔看到这里，忍不住跑出来骂两句活该！不过，网友这个错失，99%的外贸人都会犯。明明是客户自己错了，为什么说是网友的错？明明是老外自己不紧张自己的订单，关网友什么事？

以上心态，是一个典型的业务员心态。做个平常的人，拿个普通的提成就可以了。我们再看下去，网友的这种心态会在"大客户行为"下变成一个什么样的结果？

网友在最后关头收到钱了，可是已经太迟了。老外根本没有留多少时间给生产。以下便是网友的反应。我看出了很大的苦心，网友还在想办法安抚老外说迟到有迟到的好，运费便宜点。可是很明显菜鸟不知道，比起赶在圣诞节前上货架，根本没人关心这点运费。好心的安抚，很容易被反过来利用……

客户的邮件如下。

D,

We just got payments yesterday.

If to meet 12/11 sailing, we need to finish loading at 9/11, it's impossible for us to finish production of 3 containers within 5 days. I hope you can understand.

Especially at present all orders around Xmas and Spring Festival are waiting in line for production.

We have had to put off some customers' orders.

While the good news is I heard about that the freight cost will drop a lot after Xmas. And send several containers at one time can get a better discount on freight cost too.

你可能难以想象，你这样一句好心的话，很可能会变成把柄。轻则成为老外间的一个笑话，重则成为代罪羔羊：他们根本不知轻重，这样还能合作什么？人家新旧阵营在角力，当中会利用什么作为把柄……这不是没有参与过的人能理解的。

It seems that you need longer time on balance payment. It took more than one week.

I want to know if we need balances at the end of Nov, when do I need to remind you the balance payments?

网友：结果客户的采购回复仍然让人上火，邮件也抄送给了销售主管，最开始联系订单都是由销售主管确认的，所有邮件基本都是同时抄送给好几个人。

It seems that the terms are not suiting how we work if I'm honest. It is disappointing to see that out of 4 containers we wanted delivered in Christmas we are now only going to get 1. The problem being is you have our deposit for the 3 containers but we are not going to get them this year. We need at least 2 weeks notice on deposit requirements and balance payments preferably so Sharon has enough time to do what she needs to do including getting the payments authorised and signed off.

Please now send the 3 outstanding containers with deposit already paid at w/c 5th December, 12th December and 19th December so as to receive them w/c 9th January, 16th January and 23rd January 2017. You must ship a week between each container.

Please confirm you understand our request.

好了，原文停了。看到了吗？这叫指鹿为马，非常不讲理。气愤吗？气愤！很奇怪吗？以本叔多年跟老外打交道的经验，更指鹿为马的事情都常常发生。网友懂得上火，算是清醒了。更多可怜的业务员真的以为自己错了，在反求诸己呢！

现在让我福尔摩"本"还原一下故事的真相：有人故意或意外地延迟付款（当中有很多种可能性），相信那个 D 先生已经知道罪在己方了，这件事牵连巨大，中国人真的不发货了！于是他最直接的办法是让中国人觉得自己错了,反正他是大公司的买手,你敢不服?很可能他有过成功的经验,只要吓一吓供应商,别说交货,就连赔货都有可能。先来一个指鹿为马迫使你连夜加班,再赔空运,真是一个神奇无敌的"disappointing"!

我为什么说网友活该呢?因为她应该在那个准备不了了之的关头,写一封电邮,说以下这句:

Well understood. Our production will start upon receive your deposit. Pls be reminded that production lead time would be 20 days.

这招叫作白纸黑字。这是你不能用WhatsApp取代的,必须发到客户公司的邮箱。他日有什么争论,你也有理可依。跟大公司玩,就要用大公司的玩法……

这一次,本叔选择了一个十分强硬的回复。我没有办法百分之百从简单的一段例子知道网友的这段生意关系,所以我只能以供大家学习的立场出发。这样的回复,如果用在问价中的客户,那是必死无疑,但他已经付了订金就不一样了。这是一个险招,90%的情况下不太建议大家用,但是学BE不要只学范文,需要据理力争的时候,就要站出来。

参考范文如下。

Hi D,

You know better than I do regarding your company payment system.[1] I think we have

1. 他原文有好几句在说自己的付款系统是怎样的,关我什么事?

reminded you several times of the payment and I don't understand where is the confusion coming from.[1] Production starts only upon deposit and it takes 20 days lead-time to turn material into your product. I think our quotation and my previous emails have made it quite clear.[2] There is no magic.[3]

What I can do now to rescue[4] your situation is to relocate the maximum of our resource to your production even if this means to jeopardize our other customer's delivery.[5] Of course you will not receive everything per your original schedule, and will cost you extra on premium transportation in order to hit your requested lead-time.[6]

1. 这已经是很礼貌的了，他说我方不知如何与他们一起工作，我看这样回复也挺适合的。
2. 白纸黑字的力量！那些随便在WhatsApp上报个价的看过来！
3. 这句酷！
4. 不妨用"rescue"这个词，因为你真的是在帮他收拾烂摊子。
5. 懂"jeopardize"这个词吗？查查字典，美国人常用。不是那种在朋友圈流传的所谓的商业英语教的英国农村80年前的方言，像"clothes made the man""don't prop your feet up"之类。
6. 直言不可能有他想要的结果，最重要的，还是他付运费。

This is not what we want but if this is meaningful to reduce your loss we can do that. Otherwise goods will be delivered at our normal lead-time.

I guess this is the best we could do. Thanks.

Regards,

Ben

> 我是在帮他，这是底线，不要拉倒！

这次用的生词有点多，但都是很常用的，值得学习。

本部分建议掌握的 BE 金句

1. You know better than I do regarding...
2. This is not what we want but...

REALLY GOOD NEWS
YOU WANT TO EXPAND YOUR MARKET

第6章 关　　系

记得某次线下有人问,他已经比同行便宜15%左右了,为什么客户还不来跟他买呢?我说,15%算什么?你知道换一个新供应商,我的成本是多少吗?

一手坏英文，真的会把朋友气成敌人。相反，BE写得好，白不会变黑，黑却能变成灰。

在本章第二部分中，网友明明是帮客户在极短时间内把新产品做出来了，可是客户却说他发现自己买贵了，很生气。"急单的成本是常规订单的两倍"，这是我说的，难道这不是各取所需吗？这本来就是合理的事，你得用英文好好解释，说服客户，然后重新打开合作的大门。BE用得好的话，可以很高。

本章第一部分是关于一些过分的客户要求。有时我看到一些小企业不懂如何面对厚脸皮的客户，为了保持关系就痛苦地接受这些过分的要求。我明白，有时不是你想不卑不亢，而是你的英文有限，水平不够，那么加油吧。

本章第五部分是关于飞单。一个业务员离职了，准备向老客户下手，该说些什么？采购换一个供应商的成本往往比你想象中的大，而且还大不少。那么要抢单的话该怎么入手呢？

国内侵权问题严重已经是不争的事实，但不要以为这是国际惯例。本章第三部分中的网友就是碰到老外投诉，看看本叔怎么"以奇攻，以正合"。这个案例中的策略特别棒。

本章第四部分看似是一个没太大意义的邮件，只是聊聊天而已。事实上，聊生意不就是不断地聊天吗？Business Development（深耕业务）看似是个新概念，但其实我们一直都会，只是换成跟老外用英文聊时，方法又会有些不同。不要觉得这一部分是高层对话，自己用不上，要知道，在公对公面对客户的层面上，你就是你公司的高层。

本章第六部分也是同一本质的。有些铺设，能让你之后的工作轻松一些。

客户想把你的产品美照借为己用怎么办

我们做网店的做了一段时间后，对侵权这码事都有一套见解，名叫无奈。平台上的同质化不只是产品，有时连图片都是百分之百抄袭。有时我会想，如果抄袭者连我的logo都抄去，我是不是应该开心，因为这好像还算是个宣传（阿Q精神……）。可事实上是不会的。2014年我设计了一个简单又精致的喜糖回礼球，在淘宝上卖开了，很快就有一家皇冠店百分之百抄袭了包装设计，比我当时小小的两钻店高出不知多少倍的流量，很快我的设计使它卖了个满堂红，而且它开始宣称自己是原创设计。有些朋友问我为什么不投诉甚至报警，有些朋友比较接地气，表示同情。是的，我能怎样？

下面要讲的这个例子，表面上不是同一回事，但细思极恐。可能是目录做得太好了吧，老外看中了那些美照并要求"借用"，但logo要用老外的。本来大家要是好好合作一起打天下，你还可以接受，可是老外要了你花钱拍的照片后，却只跟你下了一点点订单。不是他没有订单，而是那么一丁点的订单他还要分给不同供应商。你说，这口气怎么忍？

如果他偷偷用呢？如果他必须要用原图，那你还是可以提要求的，因为必须你同意了他才会有，但如果他不在乎原不原图（要知道，差的图总比没有图强多了）呢？那他大可在你不知情的情况下用，你可能发现不了，特别是做项目的客户，渠道还是相对私密的，就算你发现了，你能怎样？上国际法庭仲裁他？在绝大多数的情况下，你不能怎样。

我们来看看原文吧。

很抱歉打扰您，看到您对别人英文邮件的分析，我很佩服。我有一封邮件，主要是关于希望客户不要拆分订单，集中订单到我们公司。可以麻烦您帮我看一下吗？

背景：因为刚给客户发了我们的新品图册，客户觉得很好，希望我们可以直接把图册上的 logo 给他换一下，在换成他的 logo 的邮件基础上答复。我们老板希望我跟客户表明，要求他们也对我们忠诚一点。

客户情况：邮件内容一般都非常简洁，非英语母语国家，比较大型的工程客户，偶尔有工程需要户外家具，在我们公司采购过几次，因为有中间人给他介绍其他的供应商，中间人收取了佣金，之前在合作的时候就有和其他工厂拼柜的情况，所以近期的订单我们预计他都下到另外的工厂去了，他的中间人也是他合作很久的照明行业的供应商。

公司情况：毕竟我们的图册真的是花费了很大的人力、财力和物力做出来的，公司还特地把新品运到海南去拍照，要知道我们的产品都是很大件的家具。所以老板觉得好像客户并没有对我们很忠诚，希望可以给客户敲一下警钟。

最后，无论如何都很感谢您分享这些干货给我们，不管您有没有时间或者兴趣解答我的问题，总之很感谢您的分享，好人有好福气。

承你贵言,我只求多卖两粒巧克力。这个例子有趣的地方在于谈判。就我所看,他来问你能不能用你的图片,就有两个可能性:

1. 君子之心,他这是尊重版权。

2. 小人之心,他是因为想要原图。

你的选择:

1. 可以威胁他,"不给我所有订单休想要图"。

2. 白给他用,无条件接受。(除非你的对手卖跟你一模一样的货,否则你还怕他不跟你要货吗?)

3. 有条件接受,"如果你……那你可以拿去用"。

可惜,单凭这个例子提供的那么点资料,我无法给你意见该怎样去决定。可能你的老板是对的,老外最后要怎么样做是他的做事方法,你控制不了结果,但你可以申明你的要求——老外你应该多给我点订单。要是你够硬,不在乎这等小单小客,那么是可以趁机威胁一番的。不过,看原文好像并非如此。

Dear ××,

I'll apply for this.[1] ××, you know we took a lot of investment including effort, time, and design on this catalog, not even mention the cost.[2] It's our baby and our proud. We are so glad that you like her.

1. 对,说会去申请就行了,情况未明用不着马上说不。这就是为什么很多老板都爱假装自己只是打工者。

2. 这些都是成本!通过这句话看到了网友对成本系统不清晰,建议他学学采购。

××, what we want to do is to have long time cooperation with you.[1] As you know we could produce different style of outdoor furniture and we make it well. Also we are responsible for our products. These made us to be the exact great supplier for project customer.[2]

The truth is that outdoor furniture covers only a few percentage in projects. And we devote all we have for you but you split the small orders, that seems not very fair.[3]

We hope you would not split your orders into different suppliers. It's also more simple for you to manage supplier.[4]

And if you have worries about anything like quality, price and production time. We can talk. We promise we'll try our best to cooperate you well.

Best Regards,
C

以下是参考范文。

1. 很中式。就算要这样写，也应该用"long term"而不是"long time"。
2. 值得一赞的是，网友提出了"专供项目客户"这个概念。有人可能觉得这没什么大不了。说与不说，已经是很大的分别了。可是网友的句子写得没高度，只能说是清晰。
3. 那么重要的点，你就一句"it seem not too（不是用 very）fair"，满满的无力感！这里要大做文章才对。
4. 这是好的切入点！

Hi,

　　Thanks for your interest in distributing our product and in particular[1] the products in our latest catalogue. Many of us agree this is one of the best album we have taken for our products.[2]

　　As you can imagine we've spent quite some cost and efforts on this catalogue, I am not sure we can just let anyone borrow the contents and put their logo on it.[3]

　　Although I understand it could be an efficient way for you to make more sales, it is quite an uncommon request to us.[4] Anyway I will bring it to my boss and seek for his consent.[5]

1. "in particular", 意思是"特别是", 这里以礼貌的形式开始, 并直接带入"目录"这条主线。
2. 夸夸对方有眼光是不会伤害自己的。"我们都很满意"的潜台词是:"你真有眼光, 这是我们的镇店之宝。"
3. 单刀直入说"no", 不要"not very fair"那样有气无力地拒绝。事实上你是有充分理由直接说不的。给你用, 是人情; 不给你用, 绝对是有道理的。记得我在前面说过, "I am not sure"是客气版的"no"吗?
4. 这里也是学问。我知道你也是想多卖点货, 这很好。可是, 打一巴掌给一块糖, 这是拒绝的艺术。
5. 不要自己说"no"。这个"no"字, 客户永远觉得只有老板才有资格说……

I believe this request would come more nature if our business relationship go deeper.[1] Outdoor furniture doesn't seem to be your key scope of business and it does make perfect sense for you to consolidate demand to one single supplier.[2]

We would like to be in this strategic position.[3] In this way we could extend our support to another level — strategic, exclusiveness and competitiveness. The catalogue would just be a piece of cake.[4]

1. 这句话高。潜台词是："也不是说一定不给，也不是说要威胁你，不过，如果我们成了好朋友，那一切都好说。"脑中想象一下奸商形象……其中这里的"come more nature"是精髓所在，"一切都来得更自然"。
2. 我把原文中那几句改为一句了，这样不一定好，因为我假设了一个采购必须要懂一些专业常识。这里有个生词"consolidate"，你可能要查字典了。这不算是个太专业的用语，意思是"集中"，物流行业常用，所谓的"consolidator"。
3. 有诚意地说：我们想成为你的重要伙伴。
4. "piece of cake"是一句美式俚语，"小菜一碟"的意思。这里是说我们要是成为策略性伙伴了，别

We are looking forward to working closer with you.

Regards,

Ben

> 说一本目录了,我们还能更好地支持你,让你赚更多钱!

这一篇中的话术很重要。同一个意思你不小心表达错了,可能会有大大的反效果。这样的 BE 就很有价值了。

本部分建议掌握的 BE 金句(学会拒绝的艺术)

1. I believe this request would come more nature if our business relationship go deeper.
2. It's quite an uncommon request to us.

客户终于发现我一直在坑他,怎么破解

在合同和法律范围内,买卖双方都会想尽办法抢夺对方的利润,天经地义,没什么不好意思的。但这种"抢",不是打劫的抢,而是智取,亏的一方很多时候也不是单纯的亏,经一事长一智,当交学费了。作为采购,在第一次买一些不熟悉的产品时,我会比较接受"被坑"这码事。重要的是,我们要被坑多久才能成为专家。只要我们懂得学习,懂得进步,这些都只是学费。成为专家,不是免费的。

换个角度看，客户虽然买贵了，但是有一样很有价值的东西，是他不易理解的——上市的时间（time to market）。如果能明白这一点，你就知道为什么客户能接受你第一次的高价。如果玩得好，远不止就卖个高价。

这个例子挺经典的。网友第一次出货时价位不错，但客户也精了，懂得采购了，找了另一个便宜的供应商。现在，网友唯有想办法补救，于是就给客户写了一封邮件。废话少说，我们来看看例子吧。

你好，

背景是这样的，这个客户是业务员通过网络开发的，并成交了一个整柜的订单。

该客户是第一次做我们这样的产品，从询盘到给我们下单，整个过程时间比较仓促。根据业务员从客户那里了解的情况，该客户经过这次采购后每个月会有一单。结果客户收到货物后，最开始还在积极给新的询盘，后来就不积极了，让业务员追问，最后得知的情况是，客户嫌我们的价格贵了，已经重新找到了新的供应商，并从新供应商那里采购了一柜。

客户购买的这款产品在去年我们给他报价时，市场基本是我们那个价位，今年5月，市场上多了几个新的生产厂家，并直接以最低价格销售，与我们以前报给客户的价格差了很远。我们在这个时候也有了低成本的一手货源，也可以满足甚至低于客户目前的目标价，所以，我在这种情况下直接给国外客户写了一封信。

虽然客户回了我的信，也告诉了我他目前所有款的目标采购价

(不知是真是假),但是我再跟进时,客户直接说因为我们第一次给他的价格太高,他有被坑的感觉。

自从看了你的BE之后,我在想,如果我可以把这封邮件写得好点,也许还可以把客户挽救回来。

Dear ××,

　　How are you?

　　This is B, manager and owner of YYY. Co.Ltd. which I established 13 years ago.[1] We have been working with company like AAA, AAB, AAC...I am pleased to write to you directly instead of July today.[2]

　　1. 这里要赞一个。直认自己是所有者有好有不好,就这个例子来说,我会做同样的选择。因为客户不理你了,你已经没什么可以再损失的了,倒不如大方地以老板的姿态来跟客户聊,最后一搏。

　　2. 刚巧那位同事叫July,后面有个"today"还是挺容易产生误会的……说"instead of..."本来很正常,但整句就不太好了。我也说不出哪里不好,但是不会这样用。

　　It has been our great pleasure to work with your company. I appreciate very much that you have offered us the firm offer and how we cooperated for the order.[3] Actually after checking your website, packing design and other small details for your goods,[4] I understand you are doing everything to put additional eco value to the goods. I am happy to see that our certificates of FSC and ISO are very useful to you.[5] Since we have been in wood and bamboo items over 13 years, I realize that such eco bio packing items are popular almost over the world. I assume your market is very promising.[6] It feels touching to me that you also do your needful for charity organisation: besides your business. Actually I also do some contribution to UNICEF every month, although just a very small portion, but I trust it is helpful for the children.[7]

3. 这句改为"I appreciate your business"就好了。原文表述得太复杂，而且让人不易明白。

4. "the packing"，文法小错。

5. 这张牌打得好，环保概念能为产品增值。网友以夸赞的口吻引出自己有证书的优势，心计得满分。

6. "very promising"用来表达美好愿景，是很好的词，但句式可惜了。此处不教文法，就不谈了。整体上很好。

7. 另一张好牌——公益，特别是对欧美人来说。有时有些社会审计（social audit）还可以加分。关于这些事，有人会说是伪善，可能吧。可是本叔一直觉得，有些事，结果比动机重要。我内心深处还是认同企业在社会上该有它的责任。网友这种写法，英文简单，却让我有很真诚的感觉。这才是BE。

We have been treasuring the cooperation with your esteemed company.[8]

8. 我一向不太建议用"esteemed"这个词，因为我想不出有什么事让你觉得客户是如此"esteemed"。这跟"dear""kindly"等一个道理。生意关系是平等的，哪用得着这种花言巧语。

Unfortunately I was told by July yesterday that you have moved your orders to another supplier because of price.[9] I understand you if I was in your position.[10] From your mail, I realise that you might think we didn't support your business from the starting point the day 1. For this point, I feel sorry you got such impression . We are making every effort to support our customer to win the market, which is our principle to run the company. But obviously from your comments, we must work harder to make our customers' happy including you.[11]

9. 记得在第 1 章第四部分中我说过"price"和"pricing"的分别吗？这里用"pricing"比"price"要好，但要是我的话会用"previous quotation"，甚至是"previous version of quotation"，这个用词特别值得讲究。为什么？这跟整个回应的策略有关。我用"previous quotation"就能给人一个感觉，"我们的报价是能变动的"。一般来说，我们采购最讨厌会变动的报价，可是如果有合理的理由、解释、借口的话，有些时候还是能接受的。这已经是个半死的客户了，不妨放手一搏，用另一套打法，置之死地而后生。

10. 这里教教英文。"If I was you"为什么要用过去式？因为这是个假设，你永远不能成为他，所以这是一个不可能实现的假设，我会用过去式。你有时候可能会见到"were"，人家也没有错。"was"跟"were"都是可以的，因为主语是"I"。

11. 这一段特别不好。说了一堆以客为先之类的话，却没有一句实际有用的。既没有解释原因，也没有提供解决方案。

In order to offer good products with better price and no downgrading quality[12], every year we put a lot of attention on bettering the supply chain of every material from main to side and we also put attention on the attention on upgrading productivity.[13] For wooden cutlery, we have just finish to upgrade our production line to raise the efficiency and to save the timber during the past three weeks. According to our testing during this week, by improving efficiency and saving timber, our cost of wooden cutlery can be reduced a lot. But during the time we made the first order, we couldn't reach it. For example, price of 160 mm spoons, now we can offer at USD16.50 /1000 pcs/carton.[14]

12. "no downgrading quality" 这个词是你自己发明的吗？改为 "without compromising quality" 会好很多。

13. "bettering" 又是你自己发明的词？不过这个好，很多美式英语就是这样出来的。我建议用 "improving"，简单直接又常用。

14. 看到这里，我就松了口气，你还是有改善方案的。可是你的 BE 已经让客人有 "bull shit" 的感觉，已经先入为主了。要知道，电邮都是从上而下的，上面的文字如果越读越让人生气，那你后面的文字是事倍功半，你要非常费力才能改变读者的感觉。不过，值得称赞的还是思维，网友以"改变生产与供应链效率"为切入点。但明白人都知道，三个星期能把效率提升到可以如此降价的水平，也是不太可能。没关系，反正大家也只是找个理由而已，这样就可以了。

In all, you need a dependable and competitive supplier and we need an reliable and ambitious customer. So I hope we can sit together for business again.[15]

15. 好！直接！不吹要做个好朋友什么的。生意就是互相需要！赤裸裸的 "supply and demand"，我个人很能接受。只要不是无礼的话，很多客户也是喜欢这样直接的。

Your quick and constructive feedback will be much appreciated.

整体来说，此篇 BE 的用语和思维都是不错的。我不想硬找些错误出来，这没意思。真要改的话，我就从第四段"We have been treasuring"开始吧。因为网友前面写得不错，以下直接写第四段，参考范文如下。

Yesterday I was told that you decided to work with another supplier due to pricing reason. It is of course a bad news for us but is understandable to me.[1] Few months ago when we started working out this project together both of us were not experienced. The first batch was made in "test-tube" — your requirement is not fully standard and we need to calibrate our manufacturing capability to fit it. We were fully focusing on your time-to-market — how soon you can launch your product into your market. No doubt that would induce a higher start up cost. Yet, we worked out all the difficulty and we made it in such a short time. Now we are running into ramp up phase with many improvements — new supply chain, new manufacturing process. It is a pity

1. 所谓话术，就是寻求双方的认同点。

that you've gone. We waste our improvement and you risk a new supplier.[1]

For us it is not a difficult product and with the improvement and experience gained from the last order I am confident that we can provide a new offer that would interest you. (See attachment.) I hope we could come back and discuss our cooperation.[2]

Regards,

Ben

1. 看到没？这招够高。这里的潜台词是：我帮你开发新产品当然是有成本的！第一批我自己都没搞懂成本，贵了一点你就不要怪我了，毕竟我没收你什么开发费用。再说，因为我，你也赚了你的上市时间吧？别以为我不懂老外你的算盘，搞不好你是明知我贵了仍要买，因为当时太急吧？最后一句是说你不跟我买，是一个双输。

2. 这里简单地把我能减价的理由概括了一下。

侵权？我打劫你家其实也挺辛苦的

不知道有这种经验的人多不多：接到不知名公司的电邮突然告诉你侵权了。我明明只是把淘宝上差不多的东西拿来改一改，要说侵权，我也只是其中之一而已，更何况老外你是谁呀，我根本不认识你，更何谈抄袭你了。

似曾相识吗？这次的题目有点深。我觉得最好还是让大家先看看例子吧。

本叔，

集团客户 A 是我们业内的全球知名大户，几乎各大洲都有其旗下公司。他们对我们的新产品感兴趣，但是说我们其中一款的设计和他们现有的很像，不希望我们卖这款。我们更改了设计后，客户 A 表示还是太像，说这种设计是他们之前首先设计并引入市场的，最新的邮件如下。

We are planning on being in China the first couple weeks of December. We will try and plan to visit you then. Once we have firmed up our plans I will let you know.

I will also be placing a PO in the coming weeks for ××that we are going to buy from you for test samples.

另一款将下单的产品。

On another point, did you understand my point about the minibar optic that it is still too similar to our optics. Using a reflective optic in a minibar is considered ×× IP. Please advise.

我自己设想回复如下。

It will be our pleasant for your visiting.

Also we are ready for your following order. It will be reliable and profitable for your project.[1]

1. 棒！得一分：针对 B2B 客户，以利为先，跟我做生意，对你来说是有利益的。不要扯什么友谊万岁,很粗俗。

I do consider and get your point. I'm not so sure about this design[2] as market is flooded[3] by this basic design and my competitor has already sell this. I believe ×× designed it and invent to market.[4] Yet, please understand we had pay for the cost of building mold.[5]

2. 得第二分:我已教过"I am not sure"是一句有礼貌的否定语,用得好。

3. "flooded",像洪水一样充斥着,用得很好,第三分。

4. 你言下之意,就是承认这是××公司的知识产权了?刚刚不是说"I am not sure"吗?

5. 负分!你是在说"你知道吗?我打劫你家其实也挺辛苦的,thank you for your kind understanding",你知道你在说什么吗?

I'm open for discussion and believe that we could find a way to cooperate on this product like exclusivity.

Thanks

请不要以"天下文章一大抄"作为侵权的依据。我挺明白,你可能真的是无辜的。知识产权这码事,有很多个坑。举个例子,凭什么潘通色板内的某一种蓝色可以获得专利而叫作 Tiffany blue?为什么几个格子就可以注册为某名牌的特色?平心而论,本叔觉得这有点不可思议,可以称为"知识霸权"!(注:我写这段话的时间是 2016 年 10 月,若他日有人宣称发明了这个名词,请大家记得本叔这个人……)可是,这不是重点!重点是什么?是法律精神!国际上既然有贸易法,我们做贸易的,玩这个游戏的,就只有一条路:好好守法。你可能只是打算在国内侵一下权,反正很多人都这样,什么时候才会告到自己?可是,现在原创者找来了,那你既然承认了侵权,你该怎么办?

关于知识产权法这件事,还有很多细节。例如专利的使用地域,同一个设计,如果老外有的只是美国的专利,那么理论上只要你不是在美国销售,那有可能并不是犯法。除了地域,还有使用领域……这些种种,我就不吹了。比我懂的人有很多。我还是回归 BE 吧。

我们先来把 B 搞定。我有两个策略。

1. 同意他们,就像网友的文字,但把那句可怕的话省去。保持开放的态度去谈这桩生意。此为"阳"。

2. 同意他们在国外的 IP 拥有权,但同时宣称自己已在中国申请这个产权,让他们觉得要是在中国做这个产品,你是唯一合法的供应商。如果他们不想有任何法律风险,双方可以好好聊聊合作。此为"阴"。

想法挺高,但实际操作是一个技术活。在此为了写得下去,我做一些必需的假设,若有 IP 专家不同意,也就当抛砖引玉,恭听良言。

以下是本叔的回复。"阳"的太简单了,我就写"阴"的吧。参考范文如下。

Great to know that you are coming. Welcome.[1] As a matter of fact, we develop this reflective optics mechanism on our own.[2] Since last year we have seen some similar designs	1. 简单地欢迎一下,不用太亲切。 2. "As a matter of fact","事实上"的意思。要打这张牌,你必须坚持自己是原

flooding in the local market but none of them really suits the end users'needs.¹ Our engineers looked into it and came up with the design you see today. After receiving your claim, we've compared the difference of our products and we come up with this table:...²

We are in progress of applying this IP locally in China with an aim to prevent other factories from manufacturing it.³

As a completely separate business, OEM service for oversea customer is always our core business. With your license we are happy

创的，而不是说我已经开模了，你能把我怎么样。
1. 你原创的理由，还是因为要以客为先！知道该怎么打这张牌了吗？
2. 这里说一下你的设计与别人的主要区别，而这些区别是别人真要告你时你用来作证据的。90%的客户是不会告你的，但要是你能仔细地分析出不同之处，那么他们更没有信心死咬你不放了。就像敌兵看到我方阵营如此严谨，一般就鸣金收兵了。
3. 重点来了。由于我们以客为先，所以我们有这么一个设计。作为原创，我申请本国专利去阻止别人来模仿，也是相当合理的。我真的不是想威胁你不能在中国找人代工差不多的产品。但如果不幸地发生了这种事的话，那我可能就要被迫行动了！

to produce this for you.[1]

Apparently we will have a lot to discuss during your visit,[2] and I am sure we can solve this challenge together.

Regards,

Ben

---

1. 我们谈的 OEM 是一个完全独立的事。只要我们好好的,大家一起合作不是挺好吗?
2. 当然了。

本叔不会写开发信,但"再开发信"还是可以说一说的

年会让我反省了一下自己在公司的角色,我希望 2017 年 Luxor 又能给大家一个新惊喜。

回顾一下,我们的大部分电邮都是被动性的,老外来一招我们拆一招。这样是不够的。这一次我想试试"无风起浪",主动出击,争取主动权。事实上按以往的经验,我比较少看到已经在合作的供应商会主动去做些什么事,更不用说发一份计划书了。大部分都是老老实实生产、出货,大家没事最好别沟通太多……这样没有什么 BD 可言。BD 是什么?

Business Development 这个概念就是有些人所讲的"深耕客户"。你们都爱找新客户,却不爱在旧客户身上多找生意。一位朋友老雷在这方面写过一些好文章。你想一想,是新客户容易信任你,还是老客户?再问一下自己,你的老客户手中是不是还有不少新机会、新订单,

只是你没有把握好？老客户要开发新产品时，是优先找你还是找别人？这些事你自己想一想，我们究竟有没有把手上已有的"资源"运用好？

这一次我们来写一个虚拟的故事。故事是一家未发迹的小贸易商在抓紧了某北美行业龙头客户之后，试图做更多的生意。发邮件的人叫 Woody，是 20 多年前一家小贸易公司的外贸部负责人，也是老板的弟弟。收件人叫 Scott，20 多年前是一家虚拟的 500 强公司 Zecker 的采购经理，也是刚刚开始学习在中国采购。我们先看看邮件。

Hi Scott,

　　Season greeting! On behalf of JY, I would like to take this opportunity to thank you for all your business and support in the last year.

我很少看到中国人会写"thank you for your business"，转成中文好像会怪怪的，可是用在 BE 中是绝对没问题的。商业关系，不要拐弯抹角找些理由来感谢。人家给你生意你又赚了钱，那么就直接说"thank you for your business"。

It has been a remarkable year for us. Your business is doubled which does not only mean to us an opportunity of scaling our manufacturing operation, but also a successful proof of Zecker's outsourcing initiative to China. Congratulations![1] What's even better is the fact that we managed to improve our business efficiency by integrating ourselves into Zecker's supply chain — the value generated per head of our resource is more than just doubled. It was a great year.[2]

Looking forward, we would like to discuss further the opportunity to support Zecker's bath accessories business line.[3]

1. 这一句看懂了吗？学英文时学过"not only...but also..."这个语法吗？不过这还不是重点，重点是双赢（win-win）。这里的潜台词是："老外你的订单多了一倍，很好，这让我们的规模也大了一倍。可是我不是只想感谢你的大恩大德，我们的成功，也证明了你当初在 Zecker 内力排众议来中国采购这一独到眼光。
2. 这是想说什么？我为什么要告诉老外我们变得厉害了？现在说的正是管理能力！这一切都是为了说明我们能够再多接一点订单。客户会不会注意到？不一定会。那你要不要写？当然要写！
3. 正题来了，"我想和你们谈谈关于你们另一条产品线的合作"。以上的称赞和铺排固然重要，但并非绝对能让你有底气

We intended to improve our design capability and the bath accessories would naturally be part of the scope.[1] Two European designer houses are contracted and I can't wait to see our new Nordic style series. Another important change is our plating process line. We will invest on both R&D and production so you could expect some second-to-none[2] finishing that support Zecker to stand unique in the market.[3] I am looking forward to discussing with you face to face, probably after the Chinese New Year.

We will be closed for the CNY soon after the new year. Let's look forward to another fruitful year.

Regards,
Woody

把话题一转去聊另一项业务。BE永远只是锦上添花，只有当你本来已具备跟人家谈判的条件时，这些话术才有机会发挥作用。

1. 我总以美好的字眼去表达这个"scope"，这是一个描述"定位"的好字眼，说是"业务范围"也行。是要做什么、不做什么的意思。
2. 译作无出其右，如何？
3. 这里用了两个理由去说服Zecker为什么要给我做这项新业务：一，我们有能力设计；二，电镀技术让产品更好看。注意，我说是因为我们品质好、服务佳了吗？我说我们便宜了吗？我说要成为你在中国的好朋友了吗？记住，言之无物，不如不说。看的人水平越高，那些虚的词语越可免去。高手过招，从来都是"少即是多"。

> **本部分建议掌握的 BE 金句**
>
> 1. What's even better is the fact that we managed to improve our business efficiency by integrating ourselves into ××'s supply chain.
> 2. We will invest on both R&D and production so you could expect some second-to-none-finishing that support ×× to stand unique in the market.

关于飞单这件事,我是如何脸也不红地跟老外解释的

飞单这件事,我做采购时还真不太知道。准确地说,我不太在乎。据我所知,飞单也有很多种不同的情境。

1. 还在公司上班,但准备单干了,把公司客户的订单转给其他工厂。

2. 还在公司上班,但客户需要一些公司不生产的产品,业务员自己找工厂接单了,没告知公司。

3. 已经离职,准备自己大干一场,想起了自己旧公司的客户。

第一种情境并不道德,所以我不会教。至于第二种和第三种,在

某些情况下不一定跟公司的利益冲突（不是说这样做大有道理，我只是说，不一定有冲突。有些老板为富不仁，对员工各种欺、各种骗，那么在不跟劳动合同抵触的情况下可以接受），我们还是可以谈一谈的。

"客户是跟人（业务员）走，还是跟工厂走"这一问题，本身就值得探讨。个人而言，要是我跟一个工厂已经很熟了，一年下来也没什么大问题，又都还算配合的话，我是不会随便就走的。记得某次线下有人问，他已经比同行便宜15%左右了，为什么客户还不来跟他买呢？本叔便高傲地说："15%算什么？你知道更换一个新供应商，我的成本是多少吗？"

你不就在你的订单上换个供应商名字就可以了吗？有什么成本？

关于转换供应商的成本，简单地说，就是信任成本。我又是派人去验厂，又是花精力去搞定所有流程，你需要明白我们各种麻烦的要求，新产品既要测验又要试产，这些都是钱！工厂业务员爱投诉，说500强要求很多，很麻烦。你们口中的麻烦算什么，其实我们花的成本一般都比你们高，而且应该还高不少。单是人员工资差距就已经很大……

所以，转换供应商的成本很大，也有风险。如果你真的要抢旧老板的单，那么你应该明白，老外最关心的是什么。

1. 诱惑要足够大。15%绝对不够。
2. 转换成本要尽量低。
3. 转换风险要小。

以下这篇例文，是某业务员发给某500强采购总监Ben先生的"飞单启示"。业务员已经离职了，准备自己成立一家新公司，希望客户把订单转走。虽然他写得不错，但并没有什么用。

Hi Ben,

As you may have noticed, I have left YYY last month and is about to start my new career. I would like to take the chance to thank you for all your support in the past.[1]

1. 用"new career"比用"new business"要好。因为"career"一词容易让人忘记你背叛了旧主这个不争的事实。"career change"总是给人阳光上进的印象，不是你说"start a new business"所能比拟的。

My new plan is to start a business similar to YYY.[2] Being in YYY for 5 years I know exactly how to do better in this business in terms of product evolution and quality management.[3]

2. 这里采取了一个开门见山的策略。一般来说这样也会比较好。当然，还是会有个别人士会觉得太奇怪。

3. 这是一个有效的说服点。我在这个公司5年了，我知道怎样才可以做得更加好。这样客户会联想到你旧公司的种种不是，这是一种心理上的提醒，同时也是一个说服力强的行动计划。

As Zecker is a very important target customer to us, we will do our best to win your trust.[4] We are a team composed by industrial experts covering different functions in the business.[5] As a very small operation, we would very much like to be a backup to YYY and to grow by constant learning.⁶

4. "win your trust" 说得比 "win your orders" 得体太多。说到底，更换供应商讲究的是一个信任成本。

5. 就算你真的是单干，也不要忘记你是一个团队。你可能会说，我就是一个SOHO（在外贸界指单人公司），一人吃饱全家不饿，需要什么团队呀？可是你要明白，团队不一定都是你花钱招来的人。你的供应商、工厂车间的工人和保洁人员都是你的团队成员，他们是不是专家？当然了！保洁人员都打扫卫生几十年了，不是专家是什么？500强最喜欢的就是什么事都说是团队，集体承担责任，很500强。

6. 这个 "backup" 最关键。你可能心很大，两年内要取代你的旧老板成为行业龙头。心，可以大，但切入要够实际。做备胎绝对是件好事，毕竟给你多了，你也 "吃不下去"。

To start with, we could offer $0.21 for part #××××which I understand is one of the Zecker's highest volume part, yet problematic. This price is almost half of what YYY offered.⁷ We are willing to absorb all the costs related to development and certify this part into Zecker's supplier system.⁸ My aim is to provide you a risk-free and zero cost alternative to YYY.⁹ What I ask for is the opportunity that you try our product. Meanwhile, I am legally possible to discuss this new relationship with you since my employment contract with my former company has ended, so it placed no restriction on me.¹⁰

7. 找一个最具标杆性的产品，以你最好的价钱切入。产品一定要够主流，最好是你和客户一起经历过最多问题的那款产品。因为这样最易入脑。客户自然会在心里比较。标杆产品也很容易在客户公司内部沟通，容易形成"他比旧公司便宜一半"的心态。

8. 吸收所有成本是句口号。我不相信客户真的会给你开一张发票，然后让你为做测试买单，所以你这样说就很有诚意，也代表你很有信心。

9. 没风险、零成本，回应了前面说的客户转换供应商最重要的考虑点。

10. 你最好告诉客户你这样做是合法的。小客户可能不在乎，但大客户一定会关心这个问题。

I hope this email could interest you. If possible, I would love to come to US and meet you in person. Wish I could hear from you Ben.[11]

11. 最后，约见面。采购人员按道理是会接受你的约见的。因为他想听听你旧公司内部的信息：反正你那么远找来的，我就听听吧。换个角度，客户要是能跟你面对面谈，那你也算是成功了一部分。后面就靠你的人品了。

Regards,

Andy

Former employee of YYY

本叔从未做过业务员，是不是真的可行我自己也不敢说。不过，这些飞单信、飞单电话、飞单约饭……我倒收到过好几次。有些是挺让人反感的，特别是那些一直在说他前老板各种坏话的人。生活不易，这个我懂，但不要太低估听者的智商。要做到不让人反感，最好的方法是"完全以解决客户痛点为出发点"。

新年第一单,不拿白不拿

"一年之计在于春",过了春节,很多业务员选择换工作。但事实上,你的客户也已在这时计划好未来一年的采购大计了,不知有多少人能把握住这个时机。这一次我们又来一次"无风起浪",撩一撩客户,一不小心,订单可能就来了。

任何一家正常的公司都会做年度计划(annual plan),而且大多数都会在年底或年初时做(当然,个别行业不同,也很难说是否都这样)。采购人针对产品和项目制订采购计划,供应链人针对淡旺季制订采购计划。也就是说,你的客户在春季时就已经想好了今年的大概采购情况,这意味着你有机会在年初时就知道自己今年的生意会是怎么样的。

采购和供应链这两个岗位我都做过,都熟悉。在有规有矩的大公司人们都喜欢按计划行事。除非实在是出现太大的难题被迫做出改变,否则一般事情都能用"We've planned this way"一句话概括。采购人员的这种心态,销售人员可以多加利用。很简单,你们在做计划时想尽办法切入,尽量多出现在客户心中,甚至帮助客户完成工作,那么你们还担心订单一时有一时无吗?再者,一个可靠而稳定的生产计划能帮工厂省下巨大的成本这件事,我已在其他文章中说过了。

Happy New Year Ben!

In our last meeting, we talked about the ×× project that would be re-launched by Q2 this year. We are all excited about this. I think it would be high time to talk about our progress.¹

1. 先找点事聊聊，最好是他自己说过的。那些领导来中国看供应商时，都特别愿意聊大愿景、大项目，而大部分都是回去后就没声音了。不要轻易放过他们！把这些聊过的事拿出来说，十分正确。

The critical resource for the technical requirement of the project will be available during Q1. We are in progress of hiring 2 engineers from Singapore. Our existing supply chain could cover 70% of the project requirements and our sourcing managers are working on to complete it. These 2 critical issues as per what we discussed are in good sharp. What we are waiting for now is your green light.²

2. 这里扯一些细节，扯得好认真。

Most of our customers are busy with their annual planning by this moment. As your supplier, we would like to see what we could be assisting you with.³ By working together we could plan our resource better, which in turn, will induce cost reduction that benefits both of us.⁴

3. 不要用"help"，要用"assist"，"assist sb. with sth."。以前香港的酒店都说"may I help you"，不知何时改为了"how may I assist you"。这是个好的改变。我有手有脚，没什么需要你"help"我的。但是你"assist"我还是可以接受的。这样说话，态度和礼貌都拿满分！

4. 以减价作为一个开聊的诱因，代价好像有点大。不过你以为你不聊，就能真的不减价吗？再者，你自己开口减3%，比客户开口减5%要好。我之前有文章写过"自动减价"的思维。不过你要是真的很怕,就不要用,找个适合自己的方法去学习。

Also we need to make an advance purchase of certain critical resource to avoid any risk of shortage.[5]

5. 这又是一个好理由。有些关键部件或原材料是要抢的,不是你想要就能马上有。这个问题,你的客户一般都比你还清楚。那么此时你们不就应该顺理成章地坐下来聊聊吗?

It would be great if we could schedule a short conference call to speak about your plan this year.[6] We will see what we can do to support you better.[7]

6. 我教过"call for action",不要就一句"looking forward to your kind reply"。

7. "We will see what we can do",我们看看能做点什么,这是一个看起来很虚但又像是很有诚意的话。

Regards,

Woody

供应商完全可以主导整件事情的节奏,好自为之吧。

本部分建议掌握的 BE 金句

1. These 2 critical issues as per what we discussed are in good sharp. What we are waiting for now is your green light.

2. Most of our customers are busy with their annual planning by this

moment. As your supplier, we would like to see what we could be assisting you with.

3. By working together we could plan our resource better, which in turn, will induce cost reduction that benefits both of us.

4. We need to make an advance purchase of certain critical resource to avoid any risk of shortage.

REALLY GOOD NEWS
YOU WANT TO EXPAND YOUR MARKET

第7章 文　　案

做 OEM 不是要当英雄，而是当英雄后面那个无名英雄。当你的客户成为人人拍掌的英雄时，你就成功了。

自从步入 2010 年，我国的营销能力有了重大发展。这一点大家应该都从每日接触的广告上深切体会到了。营销也出现了很多细分领域，如小米的产品营销、杜蕾斯的热点营销等，都是一点一滴在进步。回头一看，十年前的广告，除了脑白金你还记得什么？可是，在 B2B，特别是国际贸易 B2B 上，这一点的进步实在难以比较，最直观的就是国内的淘宝和阿里巴巴国际站之比较，大家打开网页，看看图片的差别就知道了。

我认真想过究竟是什么造成这样的分别，我认为有两种可能：一是意识问题，觉得这样就够了，不用更好；二是资源和能力问题，找一个能写英文文案的人非常不容易，不是英语能力的问题，而是文化要跟西方接轨，同时又要懂商业，还要能理解中国老板，听起来就很不易。

文案属于高级 BE，也不是读几篇我的 BE 就能学懂的。我也只是尽可能详细地做个入门介绍，这背后最关键的，还是需要你自身拥有整套的广告营销思维。国内的英文营销（marketing）人才非常之少，你的公司可能就你和另外一两个同事懂点英文，你不去学就没人写了，"拼着命去干好"吧。

网站上的"关于我们"怎么写

这次我不改人家的电邮了，来说一下英文文案。毕竟，BE 的应用范围相当广。

在营销（"marketing"，我不是说销售"sales"）上，内贸和外贸明显不在同一个水平上。看一看淘宝上的图片，再看一下你发给老外的照片就一清二楚了。文案呢？一样如此。这些年来去看展会，我收到一本又一本印刷低级，图片疑似用手机拍摄的目录，很少有一本能给我留下深刻印象。在内贸，段子手已经横行，文艺青年又重新找到了人生与职业方向；而在外贸，你还是在说你的工厂坐落在一个美丽的沿海城市，拥有××平方米的厂房，欢迎国外的朋友携手共建一段美好的友谊。差距太大了。

这一次，我们来看一家知名的巧克力企业是怎样写海外文案的，先来看一段关于公司/品牌介绍的文字。

Luxor wedding started with something sweet. Being the first to introduce this kind of chocolate as a wedding element into Asia, Luxor chocolate quickly established its awareness as a brand of wedding and a brand of love.

讲品牌历史还是有些套路的。《定位》一书中说道，要占领客户的心智，最好的方法莫过于做市场上第一个导入新品类的人。如果你真是品类第一，不要多想，马上写上。当然，咱们99%都不是这样的品类第一，那么就不要乱写了。第一句"started with something sweet"很直观，

Luxor wedding moves on[1] by creating and designing unique wedding favor and manufacturing it by our own workshop or carefully selected manufacturing partner.[2]

Our "little favor" turns out to be big[3] and hot choice even of celebrity's wedding in HK and Mainland China.[4]

As we understand what uniqueness means to every bride and gloom, customization is one of our key focus of service.[5] We proudly tailor-made almost any part of the gifts to reveal importance of the memorable event.

又巧妙地把爱情和巧克力甜蜜的共性联系起来。

1. "move on" 是个把品牌拟人化的词。"proceed" "make progress" 可能是你在电邮上比较常用的词，但这两个词容易把品牌描述成既生硬又流程多的老派企业。

2. 这个写法巧妙地说我们不是工厂，但比工厂有价值多了。

3. 中文修辞中学过对比法吗？这里 "little favor" / "big choice" 是一例。

4. 这个品牌出现在了女名星 Angelababy 和胡杏儿的婚礼上！

5. 这里又把礼品个性化的服务和新人对婚礼的独特性、唯一性的要求联系在一起。"As we understand"＝"因为我们明白"，强而有力。

Luxor wedding, the finishing touch of wedding.[1]

下一段文案是巧克力的介绍。

Five pieces of sugar almonds represent five wishes for the new couples: Health, wealth, happiness, children and a long life. This old European tradition has been blessing generations of loved ones in Europe and the Mediterranean Sea.[2]

Inherited[3] from this thousand years of tradition, Luxor evolved itself [4] to be a pioneer of the blessing confessionary industry. Our signature "The Luxor" and "Hanayome" color series[5] representing a rich range of pink, purple and red which is widely adopted by wedding ceremony since the Enlightenment period.[6]

1. 最后是一个口号。英文的口号是个非常大的学问。

2. 我们把其中一段关于巧克力的真实历史写出来。意大利人也有封建迷信之时，说笑而已，这是习俗。

3. 我特别喜欢这个词：传承。很美的一个词。

4. "evolute itself..." 字面上是"把自己进化成……"的意思，听起来好像怪怪的，但我看出了一个品牌的生命力。

5. "signature" 在这里不是签名的意思，日文应该翻译成"看板"，中文应该是"招牌货"的意思吧。

6. 连文艺复兴都用上了……不过，我已查了不少资料，巧克力在那时真的已经用来做婚庆了。

Originated from Mediterranean Sea, where sugar-coated chocolate was born, Luxor were created to gift and to bless.[1] The sugar-coated chocolate with a great selection of impactful color[2] is ideal for wedding gift and is served as[3] a key component of wedding candy bar.

Each piece of Luxor is made from cocoa grows exclusively for it.[4]

1. 为祝佑而生的 Luxor。"created to gift and to bless",修辞功夫在这里,估计大部分英语四六级的小朋友都会用"Luxor is used as a gift to bless someone"之类的表述。
2. 你要形容很漂亮,是不是就只会说 beautiful、pretty、nice,还有别的吗?电邮沟通注重理解,越简单越好,但文案就不同了。对文字的要求远远不止让人明白就够了。"impactful"是个简单的词,它的冲击力谁不懂呀,但你会懂得用在这里吗?我还是认为好的 BE 不是在背生词!
3. "serve as"的意思是"作为",也是很常用且很好用的!
4. 制造 Luxor 巧克力的那些可可豆当然是为 Luxor 而种,这是正确的废话。你再想

By using recipe since 40s from the last century[1], our manufacturing technique has been advanced to a new standard. Today our plant in the Mediterranean Sea area is ISO 9001 : 2008 certificated.

一想每日接触到的广告，有多少是这些不确的废话。
1. Luxor 在地中海的供应商是个小的家族工厂，在20世纪40年代就已经开始从事可可豆种植了。

现在再看看你们网站上的"关于我们"，觉得怎么样？我同意文案是高级的 BE，也不能强求自己要懂，但我相当肯定，好的文案能与众不同。

如何给国营老企业写出爆款英文文案

我在门徒课中讲过一课，是关于怎样写英文文案的，本章第一部分也分析了某名牌巧克力的文案。

这一部分比平常我们回复电邮相对要难一些。电邮是被动的，兵来将挡水来土掩。文案是主动的，需要用你的营销思维，要主动出击。再者，商业为先，英语为次。唯有多看，才能掌握。

有些感觉，真的是换了位才能理解。当你以为花了几百元找一位英语八级的小朋友帮你翻译那段公司简介性价比高时，客户看了这段四平八稳、资料丰富却又让人永远记不起与另一家的有什么区别的文案，当然没有然后了。要知道，文章不怕有批评，就怕没人看。文案同理。好的文案读完后会让人记住，最少有一两个点是可以记住的。

这次的例子是个不错的分享。国营老字号转型，面向国际。剧本很老了，但学习性仍然很强。

××Machinery Co., Ltd. was established in 1928. It was nation-owned and produced military products at that time. Since 1957, ×× starts to produce YYY machines. Now we are the biggest supplier for national standard conventional YYY machines in China and the exclusive "Famous Trademark of China" in this area.

这一段写得很好，画面感很强。

The company presently covers an area of 236 000 square meters. The products cover following range:

各种型号的机器。为了保密我就不公开了。

以上这部分太详细了，再说了，你有多大我没太大兴趣，也有不少人对这个数字没概念，你还不如说面积有38个足球场那么大。

With the certificate of ISO 9001 and CE, ×× pay much attention on production process monitoring.

不要用"monitoring"，这个写法很低级。要知道，品质是生产出来的，不是检查出来的。"process control/ process management"就好很多。

By means of 6S and lean production management, ××'s machines enjoy best cost and good reputation which are widely used in all infrastructure construction area. Owing to 400 workers and 88 years experience, ×× possesses the full capabilities of technology to supply full set of metal processing solution.

做 6S 给人的印象是你们有日本客户，这很多时候是件好事。最后一句也行，可以用"vertically integrated"这个词，更好一些。

在我看来，有两点是我最入脑的。

1. 1928 年已经成立。
2. 前身是国营企业。

其他部分我都不太入脑。那么，这是好事吗？这不是我说了算，而是客户。这两点大概已经给我某种印象了，例如投资很重（所谓的重资产）、技术很旧、效率不高，还有，你搞不定你车间的老员工。但你也要知道，单是投资很重这一点，对某些客户来说你就已经是个不可多得的重要供应商。所以，你碰到什么人就会有什么样的反应。门当户对永远是供求关系是否愉快最重要的一环。

然而，你能改变你的前身是国营企业这一点吗？不能。你不能改变事实，也不易改变你在新客户脑中的印象。那么你有以下两个选择。

1. 不写这一点，避而不谈。
2. 接受现实，等门当户对的客户找上你。以上的选择，差不多就是所谓的"营销策略"。

这一篇最大的优点在于把最入脑的信息放在最前面，这是一个很好的策略。大致上也把 what（你的公司是做什么的）、where（在哪里？那个美丽的沿海城市就不用写了，但最少写个城市名，人家查地图就可以知道在哪里)、which（跟 what 有点像，但详细一点，例如你做什么工艺。记住，工艺是 B2B 专业采购中一个最关心的点)、who（你们是谁，叫什么名字）都不长不短地介绍了。缺点呢？美中不足的是没有加上客户价值（customer value）和核心竞争力（core competitiveness）这两点。我会在第 8 章再次提到。

网站文案如何写

在本章第一部分我第一次谈到写英文文案的事，很多人都觉得太难了。是的，我觉得文案算得上是高级的 BE，是个专业的活，也不是看本叔写一两篇范文就能懂的。可是，全公司就只有你一个人搞外贸懂点英文，你不写，还有谁？所以，你尽量学一点吧。本叔的 BE，你学个一招半式也比花几万元报那些英文班要实用多了。

本章第一部分中的例子是以一个消费品做 B2C 的思维去写的，这对于大部分 B 端读者来说还不算是很贴切。这次我分享两篇我心中成功的 B2B 企业的文案，并加以评论，希望能更切合你们实际的工作。

第一篇例文来自我认识的一家企业，算得上是个行业冠军。据我了解，这家企业把 OEM 做得出神入化。欧美大品牌都出自他们之手，他们也有能力收购随便一家这样的大客户。可是他们坚持做"幕后功臣"，坚决不跟客户争利，在供应链上恪守本分。这样一家企业，到底会在他们的文案上如何表达呢？我们来看看。

Total solution is how we define The L Group. From design, engineering, manufacturing and launch, L provides a Total Solution to our customers helping to give them a competitive advantage in the marketplace.[1]

Founded in 19××, L is one of the world's largest and most respected manufacturers of high quality YYYYY.[2] We own and operate over five million square feet of manufacturing, research & development and distribution facilities.[3]

Our mission at The L Group is to provide the highest quality products at the best possible price. And, in doing so, to provide an unmatched customer experience.[4]

1. "Total solution"是他们主打的概念,这里完整地定义了出来,目的是提升客户的竞争力。
2. "most respected",根据广告法可能不能这样说,但面向国外的文案也就看你自己的文风了。据我所知,这家公司当之无愧。
3. 一般来说,我真不建议大家写自己的厂房有多大,但他们的是500万平方英尺㊀,那么这样一来,不说是不是很对不起自己?
4. 写"使命宣言"有另一套学问。

㊀ 1英尺=0.3048米。

这里的文字是用在所谓的概述里，意思是说，用最简洁的文字给人留下印象。"人的注意力可能只有几秒钟"这一说法似乎已经成为网络营销的金科玉律。最开头的文字，必须是最有力的。就像你快要被坏人杀了，你只有几秒钟可以反应，那么你会说什么让他手下留情呢？在这里，有以下几点是你要想的。

1. 重中之重，你要给人一个什么印象？以上这篇我的最深印象是第一段中的两个点：完整的产能，以及更重要的那句，"为客户创造竞争力"。做 OEM 不是要做英雄，而是做英雄背后那个无名英雄。当你的客户成为人人拍手称赞的英雄时，你就成功了。

2. 定位好你要给人一个什么印象后，下一步是"表达"。上一点跟你的市场策略有关，而这一点就看你的 BE 了。不要浪费在第一段写你公司的全名、厂房有多大之类的内容，要写一些能令人有感觉的话。

3. 很多人爱把自己公司的名称写在开头，既长又难读，感觉很不好。(相信我，作为母语非普通话的人，那些 Z 和 J 开头的名字真的不是太容易发音。同时，英文字母 J 在大部分欧洲语种的发音都很不同。单是这个就够让人停一停了！)

以上这一篇在篇幅上（绝不能长）和内容上都已经很好了，可是我知道这还不是太典型的例子，毕竟不是谁都有这样的条件，可以当例子学。

第二篇例文来自另一家 B2B 的服务型企业，是一家法国的检测公司，专为欧美客户提供在亚洲地区（重要吧）的验收服务。在我看来，这也是一个上佳的 BE。短短的文字把大部分的重点说了。我们来看看。

××is a global leading[1] quality control and compliance service provider[2] that partners with brands, retailers and importers[3] around the world ("where") to secure, manage and optimize their global supply chain.[4]

××performs Supplier Audit Programs, Product Inspections and Lab Testing. Clients from over 120 countries worldwide benefit[5] from web-based mobile friendly account management, fast scheduling and highly competitive all-inclusive pricing.[6]

1. 这一句可有可无，但你一般不敢不写。
2. 说明了本业或核心服务，"what"。
3. 说明了服务对象，"who"。
4. 客户价值，说明了用你来干什么。
5. 再一次说明"where"和"what"。
6. 这里说了核心竞争力。

写概述时，尽量把以下三个要点表达清楚。

"who"——你是谁。名字当然重要，但最好也能简短地提供资料，如深圳的一家电子研发生产公司。同时，"who"也是说你为谁服务。如果你觉得这是废话，那么你一定未遇到过看完整个网站都不知道那家公司是不是外销的，又或者做不做OEM的情况。

"what"——你是做什么的。这是指你做什么生意，有时也可以写你不做什么。这是所谓的范围，例如Luxor不做超市的巧克力。定位，定位，定位！

"where"——你在哪里。这是指你服务的地域范围是什么？另外，不要过分呈现，看的人一定懂。

写文案不易，唯有多看例子去学习。

REALLY GOOD NEWS
YOU WANT TO EXPAND YOUR MARKET

第 8 章 工 具

我的大学老师说：PPT 是一场表演。这句话一直影响着我。

本章第一部分是教大家写看厂报告的，不知道有多少业务员真的会在看完一个新工厂后写一份报告给老外老板或者客户，但我觉得这非常有必要。关于怎么简短地用 BE 给老外一个快速参考、一份观后感，这部分可以供读者参考一下。

研究表明，成人集中注意力的时间只有 18 分钟，要想利用好这 18 分钟，并且能够结合图片清楚地给对方传递信息，PPT 发挥着至关重要的作用。在本章第二部分，我们浅谈 BE 中的 PPT。

看厂报告之总结

写着写着，我发现自己好像更在乎文字是否简单，尽量不用生字，对于文法也不太在意（虽不在意，但也不能犯太多错误）。我的英语口语相当流利，但糟糕的是我的港式口音（在国外一点问题都没有，只有中国人才会在乎）。无生词、无文法、无口音的三无人群写出高级的 500 强商业英语不是梦，我要让它不再是梦，而是成为帮助中国出口企业的一把利器。

不少外贸人都经历过客户来看工厂。大公司经常来一堆人，而且还是好几拨。客户看工厂究竟是看什么呢？作为资深采购，我对看工厂的理由，大概总结如下。

- 看看工厂是真的还是假的。你以为一句"我是工厂"真能骗到人吗？

- 看你的工艺。这是相当重要的。一件产品有时是由好几个不同的工厂共同生产。什么真的是你自己做的,一目了然。
- 看你的品质系统。这是看得出来的。他们去样板室转转,聊聊收货,就能大概知道一点。
- 看你的车间忙不忙。不忙,就好好"宰你一刀",因为你饿单。
- 看你懂不懂开发产品(这里不教)。
- 看你怎么处理废料。废料处理得怎么样,这跟你的成本有关。
- ……

在你不知不觉间,看你工厂的客户可能已经在心里敲定很多事情了。不过,也有一些老外只是借着看厂来骗吃骗喝。这是 BE 的文章,那么我就以 BE 的角度去看这件事。这一次我没有改网友的文章,而是直接套用我自己写的。以下是我采购生涯之中一篇很长的"看厂报告"中的总结内容。总结是非常重要的,因为你的老板或客户有时一般只会看一眼你的总结,或者也不一定会看。怎么简单明确地总结,这里面有很大的学问。

An Example of A Simple Factory Highlight Report from SAOS

| A few words from a factory visit make customer feel comfortable. We know this well and on each visit we write something we observed for internal discussion and/or to report to customer. Below is a fresh example | 这段是引言,但不是给老板看的。这一篇是我在 SAOS 时,在国外媒体上发表过的一篇文章。 |

from our visit yesterday to a plastic injection molder company for a bowl and cookie stamp project.

Here is the brief output:

Factory general overview:[1] Good processes in place, clean and well maintained, assessed by BV（quality based）. However this is more of a low end supplier（so low cost）with old injection machines. Workload was very low during the visit, about 30%. They have a second factory, which we also visited, but it was a totally empty factory（no workers）.[2]

Financial situation: They informed an EBIT of 10%, which I would hardly believe as per the current workload, including lots of empty space. I think this company is declining and financial assessment would be needed.[3]

1. 什么是"overview"？既然是"over"，那就得真的很"over"，很有高瞻性，用最短的文字把你最想表达的说了。
2. 我用的都是很主观的词。"老师，写报告不是要客观吗？"你还打算提供数据给你老板分析吗？你老板要的就是你的主观描述，你专业的观点！再看看我最关心的是什么，流程、工艺，这些都是必须在报告中出现的。还有一点，就是"现场感"。
3. EBIT在很多上市公司中都会出现，也是大公司正式的KPI，大概是税前利润的意思。"为什么连这个你也能知道，人家工厂居然会告诉你？"这还得看你怎么问，你问不到的问题，不代表我问不到。至于是真是假，就看你的分析了。看

Social audit: They didn't check carefully enough our social requirements, they will read it again and confirm their acceptance.[1]

The color printing process on requested products 3 and 4 is thermal printing and it happens to work only on flat surfaces. So it doesn't work for 3 and 4 which are not flat and they didn't realize that before. Besides, the process is subcontracted, because their injection capability is quite basic.[2]

Alternatively, products 3 and 4 can be done in ××, but will be subcontracted anyway (trading process).

车间忙不忙，勉强也算是一种方法，利润与产品、市场也有很大关系。财务评估当然是要花钱的，但不是花我的钱。我的角色是站在专业角度提出分析。做不做，由看的人去决定。

1. 一般我会特别提醒工厂去了解所谓"社会责任"是什么，如果不懂，赶紧去学一学。在我看来，"sorry to say that"是一个老外强加于人的道德观念。我只能说，如果你站在"谁怕谁"的弱方，那么你还是要去执行人家的标准，谁叫你想做生意。

2. 我很喜欢用"basic"这个词，客观又客气。"It's a basic hotel"意思是说酒店很破，但至少还有张床能睡觉。这一段是关于我针对某一报价产品做的工艺审查。审查的重点

AQL: They were not sure about the meaning of this standard even if they worked for Japanese suppliers, but they are confident they can achieve it, based on samples approved by end customer. Some more focuses will be needed on the inspection process during first batch.[1]

Samples request, 2 options: Either using real samples, so cost will be the mould cost + sample cost (very expensive), or just the shape in a different material and cost will be about 100 € each (handmade).[2]

之一是工艺的能力（capability）和生产是来自机构内部（in-house）还是来自外包（subcontracted）。这些都是远在欧美的客户很感兴趣且很有价值的要点。
1. 不知道AQL，但又很自信能达到是什么情况？这个报告只是个概述，所以我提出了疑点，留待下一次品管的人去验厂时跟进。
2. 这一点是老外特别交代要了解的，所以我也跟厂家谈了。

这个报告短短500字左右，包含了工厂现况（开工不足，还算整齐）、工艺水平（达到基本要求，但很多工艺是外包的）、品质（连AQL都没有）、财政能力（10个点的利润）等。报告要尽量分点去陈述，这样也能让读者看着比较舒服。

邮件之外的 BE：简报的思路

这一次我们挑战难度，聊一下不能用文字表达的话题：商务简报（business presentation）。

我曾经批评说，不要学英文演讲。我的主要依据是，不要还没学会走就先学跑。作为外贸人和外资人，你不会有太多机会去向群众做演讲，所以你先学好被动反应，再学主动的思维……把这些都练熟后，才去学用英文说服别人。希腊人、罗马人的古代教育有演讲这一项，重点是公民教育，并不是我们职场上的"即学即用"成人教育思维。

这一次我想说的不是演讲（speech），而是简报（presentation）。简报的目的有很多，例如：

- 介绍你自己和你的公司。
- 说明一个问题，并提出解决方案。
- 报告发生过的事，并总结。

只要是你想向别人清楚地表达一件事，而你又认为图文并茂、边听边看效果更好的话，那你就可以做简报。很多人都知道，"解决问题"本身并没有"报告一个已解决的问题"那么重要，公司越大越是这样。

我在没有 PPT 的年代就已经开始做简报了，我觉得当时的简报形式更生动。为什么？我用一支笔在投影机的胶片上写和画，说到什么就写什么，"视觉服务内容"。这很适合我这种想到什么就说什么的形式。然而，大约在 20 世纪 90 年代大家都开始用 PPT——第一代的微软 PPT 真是个创新。Word 改良自 Wordstar 和 Wordperfect，Excel 改良自 Lotus123，但 PPT 并不是从任何现有产品改进而来的，而是独自成型的，成为现象级的产品。在此之前也有人用幻灯片，然而这个词就像录音带一样，成了历史。

PPT 的出现，让我在做整个简报时更规范。有了 PPT，我再也不是想到什么就说什么，而是根据一个已经定好的次序，按定好的内容去"表演"。我的大学老师说：PPT 是一场表演。这句话一直影响着我。

近年来，国内做 PPT 的水平大有进步。不久之前，还是整个页面都是文字，就算是现在，老一辈的讲师和老师仍然这样做。整个 PPT 的思维像书一样，到哪一页时就读出来，这样一来，PPT 的确是减轻了人们记忆的压力，也可能让上台的人没那么紧张，但是这就毫无表演的感觉了。

近些年另一个现象级的名词"TED 演讲"把做简报这件事推到了另一个层次，18 分钟的简短演讲风靡一时。为什么是 18 分钟？这又是另一个重点！研究指出，成人注意力的集中能力好像没比儿童好多少，我们能专心听一个人单向说话的时间是非常短的，有人说是几分钟，也有人说只有十来秒。如何利用好这短短的 18 分钟把事情说好，这是一个技术活。这一点，不管你"TED"不"TED"，都是所有简报的重点。最开始的几分钟一定要好好地利用！

以上，我们看到了两个 PPT 的关键词：表演、精炼。排除内容是否精彩（这非常重要，但跟演绎方法无关），这两个词大概可以总结

PPT的重点了。以下我回答了一些常见的问题。

Q：多少页的PPT最合适？

A：这个问题没意义。回归本质，你做PPT的目的是什么？这直接影响你的内容，从而影响PPT整体的长度。如果问题改为"向客户介绍自己公司的PPT要多少页"反而可以讨论一下。你可以想象一下这样的场景：你成功地开发了一个客户，客户向你要公司的介绍，你认为他会花多长时间看，会怎样看？除非他对你的公司非常感兴趣，否则他只会挑他想看的部分看，例如产品。在你的立场，他看的资料越多越好，因为这意味着他会对你的公司和产品有更多了解，你也就更有机会成单。所以，你的PPT一方面要方便客户查找他想要的信息；另一方面要争取让客户多看一些他不一定觉得重要的内容，这两点要同时做好。对于PPT需要多少页的问题，结论就是没有结论。不要死板地固定一个数，最重要的是要把以上所说的因素考虑进去。

Q："用来看的PPT"与"用来演讲的PPT"有什么分别？

A：当然有。前者的使用场景就像上面所说的，发给客户（或要看的人），让他自己看就完事了。PPT要强调可读性（readability），不用有人在旁边解释读者也能自己看懂。

后者是当你在台上时，你边说观众边看的PPT。这一类不追求可读性，看的人可以看不明白，因为他并非需要想象，他不能通过单独看PPT就知道作者想要表达什么。这种PPT甚至只有几张图片，没有文字。最忌讳的是PPT上一整页都是文字，解释的时候就像念课本，一字一句枯燥地把PPT上的文字读出来。

你要是有高超的表达能力，绝对可以做出两者皆可的PPT。

Q：PPT要是好看的话，文档都很大，不方便发给客户，怎么办？

A：我推荐一个网站，叫SlideShare，2012年被Linkedin收购了。这是一个存放PPT的平台，你可以把你的PPT上传到这个平台上，只发一条URL给客户。老外看到是Slideshare的链接一般都敢打开，不会担心是什么古怪的网站。它还可以连接你的Linkedin账户，这样还多一个SNS的渠道。

我们浅谈邮件以外的BE就到此为止了，做PPT又需要另外一套技巧。